Enough

Enough

The Untold Cost of War on America's Operators & Their Families

Kate Ethridge

Enough: The Untold Cost of War on America's Operators & Their Families

By Kate Ethridge

ISBN 978-1956-9-04260

Printed in the United States of America

Published by Blacksmith LLC
Fayetteville, North Carolina

www.BlacksmithPublishing.com

Direct inquiries and/or orders to the above web address.

This book does not contain classified or sensitive information restricted from public release. The views presented in this publication are those of the author and do not necessarily represent the Department of Defense or its components.

While every precaution has been taken to ensure the reliability and accuracy of all data and contents, neither the author nor the publisher assumes any responsibility for the use or misuse of information contained in this book.

Contents

Author's Note

This book is based on my lived experiences as a spouse in the Special Operations community, my time working as a contractor at the U.S. Army John F. Kennedy Special Warfare Center and School, and my years navigating military systems and civilian courts. Every effort has been made to ensure accuracy, drawing on official documents, transcripts, policies, and peer-reviewed research. Certain names and identifying details have been changed to protect the privacy of children and non-public figures, but the events and patterns described are factual.

This work was written because silence has cost too many lives. The issues raised here — combat trauma, suicide, domestic violence, family safety, and systemic accountability — are matters of urgent public concern. Families like mine have carried the burden of these failures in silence for too long. My aim is not to sensationalize but to shed light, so that other service members and their families may be spared the same fate. If some accounts are painful, it is because the truth itself is painful. Enough is enough.

Dedication

For every soldier who came home carrying wounds no one could see and for every family who carried them, too.

For those we lost and those who are still hurting.

For my children — my greatest calling, deepest laughter, and fiercest fight.

And for the One who never left me in the darkest moments,

who turned our breaking into a testimony,

And pain into a weapon against the silence.

Introduction

I saw it in their faces - months after returning home from combat.

I heard it in their words and the whispers of their wives.

I watched them fall apart when they were drunk and prayed like hell they wouldn't go home and pull the trigger.

I got the call when they did.

I saw men and families thrown under the bus and broken into pieces with nowhere to go and no one who could help.

For all the vaccines and tests and preventative medicine administered to warfighters prior to deployment, there's not one thing they do to prepare them for how science tells us that their brains will change.

The chaplains are one of the only safe places soldiers, their wives and family members can turn to after the fact.

"Measures taken" to prevent mental health decline, substance abuse, and domestic violence are a legal Band-Aid to release the DOD of liability.

Check the right boxes on the health questionnaire and you'll be fine.

Check the wrong ones and you could lose everything.

Make sure your cover story for that incident checks out.

I started researching, trying to make sense of it all.

Why our men, good men I knew before the war, were falling apart - and with them, their wives and families.

And the more I read, the more enraged I became.

I'm just an ex-wife with Google.

They know what is happening.

They know what our husbands and families are facing.

And they aren't lifting a finger.

There's a slow burning anger - like a lit fuse making its way to a bomb.

This book is that bomb.

It's time we said, "Enough.

Chapter One: Hope

They say one of the greatest strengths of a military wife is her hope. We hope they'll come home safe. We hope for a duty station where we already have friends or one that's closer to family. Maybe one that just has a reasonable cost of living and that's located semi-close to civilization.

We hope time will fly by quickly. That our kids will make it through the deployment with their mental health intact. That the transition when their fathers come home will be as seamless as we could hope for. We hope that, maybe next year, they won't be gone so much.

I hoped for so long that things would get better. That he really would get the help he needed at the next duty station like he promised. That, one day, his family would be enough to make him happy. That he would stop drinking. That he would stop getting so angry.

I hoped that if I was just a good enough mother and wife, he would wake up one day and change. That if I taught the kids to behave well enough he wouldn't get so angry at them, too. That if I stayed in good enough shape, his eyes and body wouldn't stray again. I hoped that if I just gave him my body enough, if I never denied him, it would quell his rage a little longer. That I could buy us a little more time. That it would be enough.

My hope was in a human who was so broken that no amount

of love from me or anyone else could fix him. Not an innocent child. Not a faithful dog. Not the one-night-stands or his TDY fling. Not the prestige of his job or respect from co-workers. None of us were enough. Not all of us combined were enough. enough.

But I was a slave to this hope.

The idea of an intact, happy, nuclear family. The American dream. The idea of a marriage that overcame the odds and gave God glory. A man who became a good and loving father to our children outside of just the couple weeks post-explosion I know now is called the "honeymoon phase." I hoped he'd be someone I didn't have to fear and love and absolutely revile in the same breath. I hoped he'd finally just love us. That somehow, someday, we'd be okay.

I hoped he would stop breaking things. That his screaming and tossing furniture wouldn't wake the kids. That if they did wake up, they'd stay upstairs. That they wouldn't hear what was going on. That if I just stayed quiet enough, or bit my tongue long enough, did all the right things well enough, that if I found the answers in the research I poured over while he slept, I could somehow manage to keep it from happening all over again.

A therapist told me that, even if he beat me black and blue straight into the hospital, he could still gain at least partial custody of our kids as long as he didn't hurt them enough. I hoped that if I stayed, I could protect them enough from the violence that was statistically likely to escalate toward them. I glanced at my toddler, happily watching CoCo Mellon just a few feet away, as my husband pressed his weight into the gun pressed to my head, and hoped this child wouldn't look over in time to witness his mother's brains splatter across the kitchen and dining room. I hoped that, if he did, some element of his deep subconscious wouldn't remember it.

How Did We Get Here?

It didn't happen overnight. It almost never does.
Neither of us would've been described as hot-headed by the people who knew us best. And if you had to pick one of us who fit that label more closely—it wouldn't have been Mike. He was even-keel. Almost *too* even-keel.
I remember sitting in the parking lot of a local coffee shop on one of our first dates when a group of teenagers pulled up, got out, slammed their car door into his 4Runner, and started walking off. They didn't even glance back - and they hit that thing pretty hard. He loved that 4Runner—kept it immaculate.

I was furious.

"Uh, are you going to say anything to them?" I asked.

He just shrugged.

I quickly unbuckled, got out, and strode toward them with a firm. "EXCUSE ME."

In fact, the only time I ever saw him truly lose his cool was when I was pregnant with our first son. We were at a neighborhood party and a drunk guy somehow managed to accidentally kick me in the back. It didn't matter that the two of them had been joking a few minutes before. In an instant, Mike's face flushed, and the veins popped out of his neck. It took five of the guys - all infantry or Special Forces- to hold him back - and that dude was toast if any one of them loosened their grip.

I used to think that kind of fury was reserved only for people who threatened those he loved. I never imagined it would one day be directed at them.

When he came back from his first deployment as a Green Beret, our marriage felt rock solid. We didn't have the traditional, transitioning-home stress and squabbles they warn you about. I was grateful to see his dirty clothes on the floor again. To have my best friend here to cook for and with. To sleep next to. To love. He was back in one piece after a deployment fraught with chaos, injuries, and heartbreaking losses. Mike was kind and patient and grateful to be back. My best friend was home.

It was better than I ever dared to hope for. I had worked in the Small Unit Tactics Phase of the Special Forces Qualification Course as the "bad guy" in their training scenarios. It was an incredibly minor role, but it had allowed me to live out in the woods with these men, observe and participate in the training of thousands of them, walk countless miles through the brush with them, and listen to the stories of war-seasoned cadre over late-night campfires. We sometimes talked about the impact of combat on mental health. We discussed the likelihood that all soldiers who experience combat and are psychologically "normal" will experience PTSD. We were preparing for ambush recox one day while discussing this idea. A member of the cadre stopped in his tracks, looked me dead in the eye, and said, "Kate, we all have it - it's the guys who don't that you have to watch out for."

I had already been married and divorced from an infantry soldier. I knew what falling apart after combat was supposed to look like. But it didn't happen the way I thought it would—not with some big implosion or an obvious sign that something was wrong. It was an excruciating, slow descent into absolute and utter hell. Hushed talk between wives around kitchen tables revealed that I wasn't alone. Almost every other Special Operations wife I knew at the time was going through some version of the same thing.

Nearly every single one.

What Was It?

We weren't sure. They all seemed to have a drinking problem—at least. Some had multiple addictions. Some had been blown up, some hadn't. But all of them had seen combat. All of them carried this weight, and most of them had moments where they simultaneously imploded and exploded under the pressure of it. We knew they all had "PTSD" - and rightfully so. But this didn't look like what the military had prepared us for.

This was a different animal entirely.

It wasn't flinching at a loud noise or having trouble around fireworks. Few of our husbands had symptoms that looked like the kind you read about on social media graphics on the 4th of July. Fellow wives reported horrific outbursts—explosive, unpredictable, rageful, and sometimes violent. Furniture thrown. Walls punched. Words that couldn't be taken back. Sometimes the verbal abuse escalated into physical abuse. Sometimes the guys admitted, when they were drunk enough, that they wanted to die. Sometimes they'd put a gun to their head or in their mouth. Sometimes they'd threaten to kill us in a variety of ways or just wish out loud that we would die, too. Many wives suspected or had confirmed infidelity. Even the "good" marriages struggled with substance abuse, survivor's guilt, depression, and suicidal ideation. Some became more impulsive and irrational.

They were all suffering somehow.

Then they'd pass out, wake up the next morning, put on their uniform, and go back to work like nothing happened.
We tried to pretend everything was okay, but they weren't the same men we knew before. We knew war would change

them. We knew they could be killed far away in a land we'd never set foot in by people we would never face, but we never imagined we'd lose them at home.

We just hoped that things somehow got better.

If I've learned anything about hope, it's that the only real Hope I ever had wasn't in a broken man, a broken marriage, or a broken system—it was in God. For years I begged Him to restore my husband, our marriage, our family. I thought that was the godly prayer: restoration, wholeness, healing. But sometimes even the good things we hope for, even the things that sound God-honoring, are not what He intends to give.

I turned my marriage into an idol. I turned my husband into one too. I believed that if I clung tightly enough, prayed hard enough, endured long enough, it would all work out. But hope misplaced in idols—no matter how noble they seem—will always fail. Only when those hopes were shattered did I learn what it meant to lean fully on a God who never does.

Living on false hope meant I also lived in fear. Fear hollowed me from the inside out. Fear kept me isolated from friends and family. Fear kept me from stepping out in obedience to what God was asking of me. Fear told me that trusting God might

cost me my marriage, my dream, even my life. And in many ways, it did.

But in losing what I thought I couldn't live without, I gained the One I cannot live without.

"'For I know the plans I have for you,'" declares the Lord, "'plans to prosper you and not to harm you—plans to give you hope and a future.'" —Jeremiah 29:11

Chapter Two: The Deadly Trifecta

I started researching the impact of combat on the brain and behavior of our soldiers back in 2010. My husband at the time, Jake, was an 82nd Airborne Infantry sergeant. We had known each other since childhood—attended the same small Catholic school and our little brothers were best friends. He was the guy who stood up to bullies, volunteered with kids as a swim instructor, and stayed active in the community. He was a *good* man.

He never drank but, after one eighteen-month deployment, Jake quickly became an alcoholic and eventually became violent—first toward his best friend, then his father. After his second deployment, it was my turn.

His family said they thought I could handle it.

I wish I could say I did.

The truth is, I was young, overwhelmed, and completely unprepared for what was happening to him—or to us. When de-escalating didn't work, I sometimes mirrored the chaos. If Jake threw things, I threw things. If he screamed, I screamed back—not to fight, but to break through the fog, to try and wake him up. Nothing worked. I had grown up in a home with parents who had an incredible marriage - wrote love letters together every night and stayed together through thick and thin. I didn't know things like this could happen: holes in the drywall, busted doors, sprinting barefoot to hide in the woods or a ditch, a loaded shotgun left on the couch.

That was my introduction to all of this, not through a documentary or advocacy, but survival.

And I wasn't alone. All around us, other Airborne Infantry guys—many of whom had spent 18 months at a time in combat zones—were beginning to unravel. One friend stabbed himself in his sleep and occasionally *sleep-drove*—like sleepwalking, but behind the wheel—waking up on back roads with no memory of how he got there. Another couldn't bring himself to sleep in a bed for months. Nearly everyone ran on a cocktail of caffeine, nicotine, and alcohol. Jake's staff sergeant ended up barricaded in a bathroom with a gun and SWAT outside his door.

Marriages were collapsing left and right. Something was happening to these men.

But starting in 2009, the military began discharging soldiers en masse for reporting PTSD symptoms.

Speaking up could cost them their careers. It became an open secret: if you wanted to stay, keep your job and protect your family's future, you kept your mouth shut. The mass discharge functioned as a highly effective gag order. That culture of silence hasn't gone away and even relatively new SOF (Special Operations Forces) soldiers have told me plainly: *"I'll never report anything. It's not worth the risk."*

I couldn't ignore what was happening and began digging

into research, desperate to explain the clear, devastating pattern we were witnessing in returning soldiers and their families, and with the hope of helping my own. But it wasn't enough. That marriage ended, and I promised myself I'd never go through anything like it again.

And I genuinely believed I wouldn't.

When Mike and I started dating, he was in the Echo course and I was working in Small Unit Tactics. These men were cut from a different cloth. They operated at a different tempo, were held to higher standards, and underwent more intense psychiatric evaluations. Their discipline, intelligence, sense of brotherhood, and calm under pressure were astonishing. I looked up to them like older brothers. They looked out for me and I felt overwhelmingly safe with them, even as a single, 20-something female out in the woods, sometimes surrounded by hundreds of them at a time. I thought—hoped—they were immune to what had devastated the infantry ranks.

I was wrong.

When it happened, it was just as bad—if not worse.

The first "real talk" conversations I had with other team wives were horrifying. And as the years passed, those stories didn't get better. They got darker. And more common.

What We Didn't Know

It didn't take a rocket scientist to see it—our husbands were unraveling. In the quiet of our homes, behind closed doors, it was undeniable: nearly all of them were carrying some form of absolutely rabid PTSD and leaning hard on alcohol—or God-knows-what else—to cope.

What we didn't know, not yet, was that this wasn't just trauma and addiction. It was something more complicated, more insidious.

The research was out there. I just hadn't found it yet.

What we were witnessing was the *Deadly Trifecta*—traumatic brain injury (TBI), complex PTSD (C-PTSD), and substance use disorder (SUD).

These three conditions are almost always *co-morbid*—they show up together. And they don't just overlap. They mimic, amplify, and exacerbate one another. Each one makes the others worse.

The result?

- Devastating chronic physical and psychological health consequences for both the service member *and* their family

- A dramatically increased risk of domestic violence

- A terrifyingly elevated risk of suicide—not just for the operators, but for their spouses and especially the children.

What we were witnessing wasn't weakness—it was *humanity.*

These men are the closest thing we have to American superheroes, and I will die on the hill that says they are some of the best our country has to offer.

But they are still human.

No matter how elite, how strong, how resilient—if you hit a person with a car, they'll sustain injuries. If someone drinks a glass of water, their body processes it and urinates. The body's response to war is *no different*. Repeated exposure to violence, chaos, loss, and adrenaline has physiological consequences—even when the wounds are invisible.

What we saw at home weren't signs of weakness —they were the predictable, biological outcomes of sending good men into unrelenting war. And in many ways, they were the direct *consequence* of the very wiring that made these men exceptional in the first place.

Because Special Operations units deploy more often and experience higher operational tempos than conventional forces, what I went through in my first marriage became amplified the second time around.

And what's worse? It's not just being overlooked.

It's being *buried.*

The Department of Defense and the VA have *failed* to adequately inform service members and their families of the risks. What we're dealing with isn't unfortunate—it's legally defined as institutional, and even criminal, negligence.

I used to believe faith meant being protected from the fire. That if I loved God enough, prayed enough, was "Christian enough," He would shield me from heartbreak and loss. But that's not faith—that's fantasy. It's a distortion of a few scriptures and a denial of the rest.

The truth is this: we will walk through fire. But God will walk with us. We will suffer, be mocked, and endure things that should break us—but He gives strength, perseverance, and grace in the middle of it. The fire doesn't destroy us; it refines us. It shapes us into the people He needs us to be for those around us.

Our God is not distant. He is a just God, near to the brokenhearted, defender of the poor and oppressed. He met me in the pitch-dark places

where I couldn't see two inches in front of my face. Looking back, I know I couldn't have made it through on my own. I don't even know how I'm here writing these words—except for God.

And He is not only the God of comfort—He is the God of power. The God who stood with David before Goliath. Who drowned the Egyptian cavalry in the Red Sea. Who brought down the walls of Jericho. Who overturned tables in the temple when His people were exploited.

These stories—mine, the operators who spoke up, the families who whispered, the caregivers who fought within a broken system—they are arrows. They point to the truth. And the Truth cannot be hidden from a warrior King.

"For there is nothing hidden that will not be disclosed, and nothing concealed that will not be brought to light."

– Luke 8:1

Chapter Three: PTSD Beyond the Infographic

Mike said the man he killed was running to kill his friends—and he wasn't going to let them come home in a box. He wasn't remorseful. Just matter-of-fact.

One of the guys I worked with in the field had pulled Mike to his team during the latter part of his first deployment as a favor to me. I was grateful, knowing my husband would experience combat under the supervision of someone I trusted fully—someone who would truly look out for him. No one ever wants to send their spouse to war, but he was going and this was the best-case scenario.

Working in tactics gave me a much better understanding of military culture and what my husband's job entailed. Truth be told, I didn't worry much about him: he was with the best people with the best training and equipment. All I could do from our little farm in North Carolina was pray. It was in God's hands, and I felt grounded through that deployment. Eventually, the guys went out to do what they were trained for.

What I didn't realize was that his calm detachment—what I

took as strength—was actually hyper-compartmentalization and a hallmark of PTSD.

The storm had already started forming.

It started with a few raindrops: disconnection, and difficulty getting through to him. He started drinking more and spending less time at home. I tried to gently address normal marital issues, but if he was in a good mood, I ruined it. If he was in a bad mood (which wasn't always apparent), I should have known better. I wasn't Southern enough. I wasn't sweet enough. And even if I sugarcoated an issue beyond recognition, there was no winning (communication and resolution). All I could do was sit there, swallow it, and pretend everything was fine—or risk an outburst.

At one point, he told me, "Unless you are completely and overwhelmingly happy with every aspect of your life, I am miserable with you."

I stood there, jaw dropped, and quietly responded, "But that's impossible. I'm human. I'll always be imperfect and have hard days."

He shrugged. "I know. That's just how I feel."

When I tried to compliment him, he interpreted it as an insult.

One Sunday, I asked if we could go to church together. We used to attend regularly but he seemed to be drifting. He didn't want to go—again—so I didn't push it. Something in him had shifted. I didn't want him to see me cry and quietly went to our room. A few minutes later, he came in to grab something. He saw me - I'm not one of those girls who looks cute when they cry. There was no hiding it. He stared at me - irritated—almost disgusted.
"Why are you crying?" he snapped.

I looked down. "I just want my husband to pray with me."

His eyes went nearly black. He contorted his face and mocked in a high-pitched voice, "I jUsT wAnT mY hUsBaNd tO pRaY wItH mE."

Then he started yelling: "PRAY BY YOURSELF. I AM NOT RESPONSIBLE FOR YOUR RELATIONSHIP WITH GOD."
I knew that. I wasn't asking him to carry my faith but to share it again - like we used to. But countering his anger would only escalate the situation, so I got up and started the

laundry.

The strippers were just the beginning—not just because he said he wanted a Christian marriage, but also because he was spending so much money on them while I was scraping by and cutting my hair to stretch our budget. When he'd go dark on work trips and I'd spiral, he'd accuse me of being insane. He told me he had to go to the clubs to be "all things to all men," as the Bible commanded—but the bank statements suggested he wasn't just a presence there, let alone a holy one.

And then he had an affair on a training mission in one of the -stans.

The trip started off rocky. He left the day after my 30th birthday while I was actively miscarrying our second child. He was distant at first and I figured it was how he was coping with grief. Things eventually smoothed out, he came home, said nothing. Mike seemed to be back to the good, kind, loving husband I married. I thanked God, and we tried again for another child.

When she eventually reached out to me, I was already six months pregnant.

Mike admitted he'd taken off his ring as soon as he boarded the plane. He said I made him miserable. That I had pushed him into having an affair. That, ultimately, it was as much my fault as it was his.

We decided to try to work through it. I was going to need another c-section, and suddenly moving back home to the D.C. area—while heavily pregnant, with a toddler, and no strong career path—wasn't a good option. I clung to stories of redeemed marriages that had survived infidelity. We could get through this with God.

But when I had a bad day—not angry, not lashing out, just sad or heartbroken—he'd accuse me of punishing him. I tried to hide my hurt to shield him from it—but he always sensed it. I tried to explain that it felt like he had ambushed me, hit my legs with a baseball bat and shattered them. I had forgiven him, but that didn't mean I wasn't still in pain. It didn't mean I could suddenly walk. It definitely didn't mean that I wanted him to hurt, too.

It didn't matter.

Then, he really began to spiral. It didn't seem to matter what

I did—nothing could keep him from finding fault and exploding.

Our second son was due soon and I had a splitting migraine. A friend of his had just graduated from a career course and was throwing a party. I wasn't in any shape to go, but I encouraged him to attend for the both of us and genuinely meant it. I only asked that he come home afterward. He promised he wouldn't stay more than an hour or two.

Four hours passed, and he was hammered when we finally spoke. I was frustrated, in pain, and utterly exhausted—but I told him to stay where he was. The last thing anyone needed was for him to hurt himself, hurt someone else, or end up in jail.

The next morning, I wrote a letter and calmly explained why I felt disregarded—not just because of that night, but because of a growing pattern of broken promises and emotional disconnection. I believed that written words, free from tone or tension, couldn't be twisted.

He picked the letter up off the table and walked to the bedroom.

Moments later, I heard screaming. He came raging down the hallway—letter in one hand, trashing the house with the other. Then he stormed into the front yard, pulled his pants down, and violently wiped himself with the letter—still screaming, in full view of our two-year-old.

Then he hurled a mason jar at me. It hit the post next to my head and shattered—glass exploding into my hair, my mouth, my dress, and my eye. My arm was cut. Blood streaked the front door frame—ten days before our second son was born.

I had learned not to match the energy of someone in this state from my previous experiences, but still, nothing worked. Avoiding eye contact didn't work. Speaking gently didn't work. Silence didn't work. The only thing that offered any hope of diffusing him was physically leaving the space. And even then, he'd come after me—through hateful texts, voice messages, and threats.

I began recording his outbursts, or "rage fits," with the hope of bringing them to a couples therapist. Maybe they'd decode what I was doing wrong. Maybe they'd agree there was nothing I could do.

But we never made it to counseling. He said he didn't have time. He didn't want to risk his spot on the team.

By the time he left Special Forces to pursue Special Operations Aviation—just three years after joining the regiment—he had put a gun to his head, pointed one at a neighbor, and waved one during a road rage incident.

On New Year's Eve of 2017, he asked me to wake him up to help with the baby, and so I did. He flew into a rage, flipped the coffee table, grabbed my hair, and pulled my head back as he threatened to open my brains with a beer bottle - while I held our four month old.
At that point, I stopped recording for therapy and began documenting in case I didn't survive.

What We Didn't Know

Most people's understanding of PTSD comes from social media infographics—simplified, sanitized, and incomplete. But what our community is dealing with often isn't the kind you can summarize in a 60-second reel. And it can be exceedingly dangerous.

They call it PTSD, but PTSD is usually tied to a single event—

a car accident, a rape, an IED blast. What our operators are facing is complex PTSD, or C-PTSD, which develops after prolonged exposure to psychological and physical stress. (Herman, 1992; Cloitre et al., 2014).

Bad news: combat involves both.

Worse news: C-PTSD is significantly harder to treat than "standard" PTSD.

Possibly the most devastating news: Combat-specific PTSD is more dangerous to veterans and their families than any other form of PTSD.

(Side note: I'm going to refer to it as "PTSD" in the sections that follow. Unfortunately, that's still the language used in most clinical research—but it's not an accurate reflection of what these men and their families are experiencing.)

The VA has stated that combat veterans with PTSD are 4x more likely to commit suicide.

A 2016 study published in the *Journal of Interpersonal Violence* (Teten et al.) states:

- "Veterans with PTSD displayed higher levels of anger,

hostility, and impulsive aggression—including intimate partner violence—compared to both veterans without PTSD and civilians with PTSD."

- "Emotional dysregulation fully accounted for the relationship between PTSD and impulsive aggression."
- "PTSD symptoms had direct relationships with both verbal and physical aggression."
- "Most veterans with PTSD engage in impulsive aggression."
- "Veterans not meeting current PTSD criteria often present with subthreshold PTSD—which has comparable outcomes in terms of aggression."
- "65% of men endorsed at least one episode of uncontrolled anger or physical aggression in the past 6 months. 14% reported such incidents daily."

If these studies are correct—and given how many confirm the same conclusions, I think it's safe to say they are—then PTSD is a far bigger issue for our war veterans and their families than the VA or DoD have publicly acknowledged.

For the Special Operations community, repeated exposure

makes symptoms worse. Research has identified a dose-response relationship between trauma and PTSD. Kind of like the longer you stand in the sun, the more likely you'll be burned, and the longer you sit there after you burn, the more significant it will damage your skin. Essentially, the more frequently they're deployed, the more the damage compounds - and Special Operations units are deployed more than any other in our military.

Imagine being hit by a car once. Now imagine it reversing and running you over again and again. The injuries compound. So does the trauma. Even if it doesn't show up on a scan, the damage is there—in neurotransmitters misfiring, in rerouted neural pathways, in overloaded processing centers.

What's broken isn't just tissue. It's impulse control. Emotional regulation. Threat response. Reward-seeking behavior. These men are walking around with rewired brains—and many of them don't know it.

As researcher Meg Olmert said in an interview, "PTSD damages the social brain network. You tried to kill people. People tried to kill you." After that kind of trauma, the brain sometimes sees anyone outside of their warrior "clan" as a threat - sometimes even their own family members. Multiple studies confirm the link between combat-specific PTSD and domestic violence—a link the DoD and VA have criminally failed to disclose. A 2005 study (Marshall, Panuzio & Taft) found veterans with PTSD were approximately **three times** more likely to perpetrate IPV than those without.

And other studies have found that men who commit acts of domestic violence are significantly more likely to die by suicide. *(Knipe et al., 2024; Kafka et al., 2022; Graham, Kafka, & AbiNader, 2025).*

Another symptom rarely discussed anymore is **alexithymia**—a extreme form of hyper-compartmentalization of emotion, seen often in Special Operations Forces soldiers after repeated exposure to combat *(Frewen et al., 2008; Helmreich et al., 2011)* that leads to the kind of implosions I've heard reported from wives across units. They're selected for this trait - at least partially. We'll discuss selection criteria in another chapter, but here's what matters: Imagine your hand is numb. Now, someone asks you to put on a blindfold and test the temperature of water on the stove. You wouldn't feel anything—until you're burning. That's what's happening emotionally. By the time many of these guys register what they're feeling, they're already boiling over. That's what leads to extreme outbursts - and the research documents it well.

It doesn't make it okay, or even excusable, or mean that we should normalize soldier suicide, domestic violence, or any manner of the third-order effects of the changes that occur in their bodies and brains - but it does make sense.

PTSD doesn't just manifest as anger or outbursts—it rewires the brain's ability to process information, respond to stress, and interact with others. Veterans with PTSD often experience memory loss, executive dysfunction, paranoia, sleep disorders, and chronic health problems *(Sherin & Nemeroff, 2011)*.

In PTSD, the nervous system can remain locked in a prolonged "threat mode," keeping cortisol and adrenaline levels elevated long after the danger has passed. This sustained stress response fuels chronic inflammation and increases the risk of cardiovascular disease and autoimmune disorders—making PTSD not just a mental condition, but a physical one as well *(Yehuda et al., 2015)*.

Most veterans I've spoken with didn't suffer from just PTSD. They also had a traumatic brain injury. And many of them turned to alcohol or pills just to cope with the noise in their heads and the emptiness in their bodies.

The hard truth? These conditions look alike. TBI and PTSD both can cause rage, confusion, poor memory, nightmares, impulsivity, and disconnection. Add substances to the mix and you're left wondering: *Which came first? What's driving the behavior? And how can we treat it when it's all so tightly tangled together?*

Clinicians call them "co-morbid," but for many of these men, there's no "co"—they're all just one monster with three heads.

There were so many nights I cried until my throat burned—screaming out to God, angry, afraid, abandoned, isolated, and in danger from the very person I should have been able to turn to first for protection. I begged Him to see us. To hear me. To rescue us. And still the violence raged. Still the silence outside my walls stayed deafening.

And yet—He was there. Even then. Not with noise or thunder, but with presence. He reminded me:

He, too, had been betrayed, mocked, beaten, murdered—by the very ones He came to save. He knew what it was to feel forsaken.

I wasn't alone. He sat with me in my horror and grief—and He grieved with me. Not shouting over the chaos, but steady beneath it. Not stopping the world from collapsing, but holding me as it did.

The evil wasn't only inside my home. It was in the silence outside of it—in the systems that turned their heads. Not just from me, or Mike, or my children, but from countless operators and families we knew—and countless more we would never meet.

But God never looked away. Not once.

What man meant for evil, He still bends toward redemption.

"What you meant for evil, God meant for good—to bring about this present result, the saving of many lives." —Genesis 50:20

Chapter Four: Hearts + Minds

We didn't know it then, but he had likely suffered multiple concussions. His paycheck even included a line item literally called "Demo Pay." I couldn't say exactly when the injuries began or what effect they had on him—or on us—but I remember raising the possibility that a TBI might explain his spirals.

He dismissed it. He hadn't been blown up, after all. Compared to friends who had survived catastrophic blasts—one even took an RPG to the face—he didn't think he counted. I wasn't sure either. We weren't given any information about the risks.

Other spouses whose partners had experienced visible combat trauma often reported abrupt behavioral shifts. But many of us witnessed something slower—a quiet unraveling. One that research now confirms is all too consistent with what's happening to the brains of our warfighters.

When he left Special Forces, we moved to Alabama so he could attend flight school and attempt a return to Special Operations as an aviator. We both thought stepping away from team life might help.

I didn't know rotary aviation could be just as brutal on the brain.

The rage continued. The cycle of everything-is-wonderful → disconnection → implosion/self-destruction only deepened.

He filed for divorce and told me he wanted to wait for someone younger, better. Or maybe, he said, we'd get back together someday—when he calmed down. He withdrew from the family and moved in with another student in flight school. Friends and family saw a version of him we didn't recognize—charming, composed, and collected. We lived with someone else entirely.

Our young son, after yet another unanswered call, said quietly, "I don't think Dad cares about us."

Two weeks before the divorce was set to be finalized, he reached out. He said he had lost his mind, that there was no way to rationalize the thoughts of a crazy man, that he was sorry—and if I gave him a second chance, he would spend the rest of his life making it right.

The divorce was paused, and I eventually—hesitantly—agreed to try again, but only with legal protection in place. The best thing for our boys was a home where their father was present and healthy, after all. I had seen the studies regarding sons raised without "a man in the home"—and they weren't good. If this was a real shot at giving them that, I had to take it.

After graduating flight school, he received a medevac assignment at Fort Bliss—an important step closer toward his goal of joining the 160th.

At first, things felt better. He was present and patient. We bought a fixer-upper in the West Texas desert. I unpacked and made renovation plans. He began integration with his new unit.

Before he signed the post-nup, he insisted that pictures and recordings of past abuse I had taken be deleted. And though I had never threatened him with them, he said he didn't want to feel like it was "held over his head." We had already moved to Texas, and if he became abusive again, the post-nup agreement covered that.

The record was gone. The promise was made. He signed the paperwork.

We renewed our vows quietly in the living room. He deployed shortly after.

When he came home? It was worse. So much worse.

At the time, I believed I had just witnessing trauma, stress, and adjustment and a drinking problem. I had wondered how brain injury could have impacted his behavior, but no one talked about it. I also didn't yet understand the personality and family of origin dynamics that would later come into sharper focus, or how some traits not only slipped through selection but were rewarded by it. That's a different chapter.

What We Didn't Know

It doesn't take a massive blast to damage the brain.

It's estimated that 85% of SOF soldiers sustain TBIs from training alone—tens, even hundreds of micro-concussions caused by blast wave exposure (BWE). Not from one major hit, but from repeated force: door breaches, firing an M4, even parachute jumps. Each shock reverberates through the blood vessels, subtly injuring the brain—even with and despite protective gear.

Even when only the torso absorbs the blast, the force still travels through the bloodstream, impacting the brain's delicate structures. That means even operators who never saw combat—but trained repeatedly with breaching charges or heavy weaponry—are at serious risk.

It's like shaking an egg: the shell might be intact, but the yolk inside eventually becomes scrambled. Over time, the damage adds up.

And many of them—many—also survived multiple IEDs or direct blows to the head while deployed. One infantryman I interviewed estimated he'd had 30–40 concussions. That number isn't unusual for "Big Army" guys who were running missions at the height of the wars.

If that's the baseline, imagine the toll on Special Operations soldiers with more frequent and prolonged combat exposure.

When I asked what kind of care was provided after suspected head trauma, the answer was almost always the same:

"None."

"It's almost never reported."

One former operator told me that in his entire career—nearly 20 years in Special Forces—no post-concussive care was ever offered after a suspected TBI.

When Mike was accepted into the 160th, we moved to Tennessee, and I started to become close with other wives in the community. As they opened up about their home lives, they reported identical behavioral issues—the same rage fits, drinking, infidelity, and self-implosion cycles I and other team wives had experienced. Air operators began opening up with their struggles too—the same exact issues: anger, suicidal ideation and attempts, drinking problems, *ad nauseam*—that the team guys were experiencing.

Even ground operators familiar with the research found this confusing.

"But ....they're in a helicopter?"

Exactly.

Research now shows that blast wave exposure (BWE) from firing heavy munitions on the ground can cause cumulative, catastrophic brain injury over time. Firing from the confined space of a helicopter cabin adds significant overpressure, creating the potential for even more severe neurological damage *(Mehic et al., 2021).*

They also receive incoming fire: RPGs, missiles, small arms—you name it. And small arms fire, if it penetrates, can kill the crew inside. Some of the air operators, particularly crew chiefs, have as many confirmed kills—and some far more—than ground guys I know.

Training accidents and deaths are highly traumatic and not uncommon: imagine watching one of your best friends fall to his death, crash or drown - and there was nothing you could do.

PTSD is a known and discussed concern. But blast-wave-induced TBI? For anyone outside of DAPS? No one is talking about it. The men I've raised this concern to hadn't even considered it.

And this isn't just about memory loss or balance issues. TBI affects everything.

It often starts with subtle cognitive symptoms: forgetting simple tasks or losing track of time. Struggling with planning. Getting frustrated more easily.

Then it progresses: irritability, paranoia, withdrawal, reckless behavior, depressive states, disproportionate emotional responses, heavier drinking. (Hayes et al., 2016).

Now-medically retired operators I've known personally have suffered from vertigo, migraines, executive dysfunction, sleep disruption, emotional volatility, and alcohol dependence—leading to the loss of marriages and even their careers.

TBI is also strongly linked to violence and crime:

- Civilians with a history of TBI are 2–3x more likely to engage in violent behavior than those without. *(Farrer and Hedges, 2011, meta-analysis of 17 studies)*

- Aggression occurs in up to 33–71% of people with TBI, particularly with moderate to severe injuries. *(Tateno et al., 2003; Kim et al., 2007)*

- Impulse control problems are a well-documented consequence of frontal lobe damage in TBI and are strongly associated with verbal and physical aggression, domestic violence, and even road rage *(Grafman et al., 1996).*

- In one forensic study, **60% of domestic violence perpetrators** were found to have a history of traumatic brain injury (TBI) *(Farrer et al., 2012).*

- In a separate study of military veterans, sustaining a TBI was associated with a **twofold increase** in the risk of committing domestic violence *(Pardini et al., 2013).*

- Veterans with both PTSD and TBI were **three to four times more likely** to report aggressive behavior compared to those without either condition *(Bryant et* *al., 2015).*

Several operators I interviewed—and many more I quietly observed—disclosed struggles with substance use, emotional outbursts, and self-sabotage following repeated blast exposures.

- In one study, **24% of patients** with traumatic brain injury exhibited serious behavioral disturbances *(Timmer et al., 2015).*

- Behavioral health disorders are **twice as likely** after a traumatic brain injury (TBI) than after an orthopedic injury *(Ștefan & Mățhe, 2016).*

- Traumatic brain injury (TBI) is **frequently present** among perpetrators of domestic violence *(Mosti & Coccaro, 2018).*

And the effects are compounded by trauma.

PTSD and TBI often occur together, and it's nearly impossible to tell them apart—especially when substance use disorder (SUD) is involved. The symptoms mimic each other. They feed each other. And eventually, they spiral into something nearly impossible to untangle.

One study found that when soldiers suffer from both mTBI and PTSD, symptoms are significantly more severe than in either condition alone. Even more heartbreaking:

- Individuals with a history of traumatic brain injury (TBI) are **twice as likely** to die by suicide compared to those without TBI *(Fralick et al., 2019)*.

- Veterans grappling with a combination of the deadly trifecta face dramatically elevated suicide risk—a dark synergy that accelerates death by suicide. In one large-scale study, those with both TBI and SUD died by suicide **63% sooner** following deployment than their peers, underlining the urgent need for integrated, early intervention *(Brenner et al., 2023)*.

Every single operator I interviewed, regardless of whether they served on the ground or in the air, disclosed serious suicidal ideation while in service. Many had held a gun in their hand—or in their mouth—at some point.

> *"Three guys from my training squadron committed suicide in the last year alone," an operator told me. "We're dropping like flies, Kate. What is happening to us?"*

This isn't rare, or isolated, or just a couple guys here and there. It's a predictable response to combat and brain trauma without appropriate education and intervention. And we *do* know why it's happening. **The DOD just isn't disclosing it.**

While recent research suggests 85% of ground operators suffer mTBI (Yurgil et al., 2020)—and based on what we know about how munitions impact the brain—I believe that after a certain amount of time in service, nearly all of them sustain some form of TBI—even and especially air operators.

Not from a cinematic explosion. But from ripple after ripple of invisible trauma—compounding damage that slowly, quietly rewires a person's brain.

Not all at once.

But gradually.

Like a dimmer switch.

Like a pot of boiling water.

We're not imagining it. Spouses and kids are watching neurological trauma play out in real time—without warning, support, or understanding. And worse still: service members suffering from mTBI often couldn't and can't see it.

Most patients with TBI aren't able to recognize deficits in cognitive and executive function. And many certainly aren't able to recognize the volatility, the spirals, the changes in behavior.

A Dartmouth study by Dr. Laura A. Flashman found that up to 45% of patients with severe TBI have reduced or no awareness of their own deficits.

That's devastating—for them, and for their families.

It's like watching someone start to limp. Over time, it becomes worse and worse, but they're so busy with work and life that they don't even notice it. You beg them to see a doctor—but they swear they're walking fine.

And when you're married to someone who insists nothing is wrong—while everything feels wrong—it starts to erode your grip on reality.

You stop talking.

You question your own sanity.

You become someone you don't recognize.

"Mom, you were a robot," my son once told me.

He wasn't wrong. I had gone numb. I gave everything I had and was trying to change the ending.

But for most of us, the ending had already been written.

One of the hardest parts was that no one else could see it. At work, he was cool as a cucumber—calm, reliable, the guy you could count on in chaos. They called him "Hollywood." He had the smile, the charm, the confidence. To the outside world, he was steady.

At home, we were drowning. Rage. Drinking. Implosions. And because no one else saw it, speaking up felt impossible.

That's when the doubt crept in: If he's this way only with me—does that mean it's my fault? Did I change him? What am I doing wrong?

I turned that question into a religion. Countless therapists, counselors, self-help books, endless conversations—I dissected every flaw in myself. Because it was almost comforting to believe I was the problem. If it was me, then I could fix it.

There's a saying that it takes two to make a

marriage fail. It's wrong. It takes two to make a marriage work. But if one person is rowing while the other is swinging an axe at the boat, it doesn't matter how skilled the paddler is. That ship is going down.

Admitting that his spirals weren't my fault also meant admitting they weren't in my control. And I wasn't ready for that. Control—even warped control—felt safer than surrender. So I clung to it. I believed in God, but I didn't trust Him with the reins. Not yet.

"We are hard pressed on every side, but not crushed; perplexed, but not in despair; persecuted, but not abandoned; struck down, but not destroyed."

—2 Corinthians 4:8–9

Chapter Five: The Flame and the Fuel

It's a little like gasoline and Styrofoam. You see them around enough—there's probably both in every home. But when you mix the two, they become something indistinguishable from either original substance—and far more dangerous. It's essentially homemade napalm, which is bad enough. But when you strike a match—like SUD—and throw it into the mix, the result can be deadly.

Deployments were always pretty easy for us. I used to tell younger wives: you'll have challenges in your relationship during a deployment just like you would if he were home. What matters is how you choose to handle them and move forward. You'll have disagreements whether he's gone or there. You'll have bad days when nothing pans out the way you want or need it to no matter what. The difference is that you're doing it apart—experiencing different things—but that gives you more to talk about. More to lean on each other for. It can strengthen your relationship—if you let it.

The distance always helped us. The boys and I were out of his line of sight. The daily friction was gone. He made an effort to stay close. He called nearly every day. We sent texts, memes, and jokes. At least once a day, we'd video chat so the kids could see his face.

When he came home from his first rotary pilot deployment, things felt good. He taught the boys firearm safety with Nerf guns. We worked on house projects. Took walks in the desert with our dogs. Cooked together. Drank morning coffee. Folded the extra laundry. It all felt soaked in gratitude.

But it didn't last long.

Shortly after he returned, we found out we were expecting again.

I'd always been open to more kids, but he never wanted three. Two had already overwhelmed him. Even before this deployment, the shrieks and chaos of toddlers triggered his anger—back in North Carolina and Alabama.

I was scared. What if he blamed me? What if he thought I got pregnant on purpose? What if he resented me? He had told me before that pregnant women weren't attractive to him—not even me. Even though I stayed small during pregnancy. We went maternity clothes shopping during my first pregnancy. He covered his mouth and said he was going to throw up when I tried on this belly that shows what you look like when your baby grows.

I told myself some guys were just like that.

But deep down, I wondered:

Would this push him toward another affair? Would he go back to who he was before?

Weeks passed.

Mike eased into the idea of welcoming a third child and

started to celebrate it, but he was simultaneously becoming listless. The 160th packet he'd been eager to submit when he got home sat untouched.

One day, as we brought in groceries, he stopped and looked at me.

> "I have everything I could ever want," he said. "A beautiful house, wife, and two sons—with one on the way. I can walk into the grocery store and choose from ten different kinds of orange juice. I can order any pizza I want and drink a beer with. But something's off. Something's wrong with me. I don't know what it is."

My heart broke.

I didn't know about blast wave exposure yet. But a counselor in Alabama—a retired SF Colonel and friend of Nick Rowe's—had explained part of it once. High-stress environments rewire the brain. It's like nicotine. When your brain gets a chemical hit from outside stimulus repeatedly —combat, adrenaline, intensity– it stops producing its own. The traumatic environment becomes your body's new baseline for normal endocrine and brain function - and it takes months for your mind and body to re-adjust.

You come home and the normal stuff doesn't register. The nervous system is starved.

I tried to explain that to him. That his brain and body just needed time to recalibrate.

He sighed, shrugged, and walked inside.

Then the drinking started.

First, just one with dinner. Then two or three. That merged into a few during the week. Then I started finding single-shot bottles under the bed. Wine cartons in the truck.

There was a pattern. The more he drank, the closer we got to implosion. He wasn't always drunk when he snapped—but the snaps almost always came within 48 hours of heavy drinking.

And the explosions came.

I thought if he could just stop drinking, we'd be okay. His rage - the things he lost it over - made no sense. There had to be a reason.

Once, the boys and I rescued a feral puppy from the desert. She had explosive diarrhea in the crate. We brought her home to clean her up. I posted a last-ditch plea on Facebook to find her a home before we took her to animal control. A CW5 Mike worked with said she'd take her.

While I ran to the grocery store, Mike let her out. I had asked him not to—she was feral. She ran off. He lied and said she broke out. Then he berated me. Said I'd ruined his day. That it was my fault. That he started drinking again because of this. That was my fault too.

I checked the crate—no damage. Then I reviewed the security footage. He'd opened it.

Therapy was stripping away the fog of gaslighting, and the more boundaries I set, the worse things got. That night, I held my ground and called him out. He snapped—threw water on me "because I can't punch you in the mouth." I turned to walk away, and he blamed me—again—for his drinking.

"You've already had three beers," I said, fed up.

"I WILL "F" ING KILL YOU," he screamed.

I walked away.

Later, I came back to grab my keys. He had been blowing up my phone. I hadn't responded.

"If you tell anyone I have rage fits, I'll "f" ing kill you. If you screw up 160th for me, I'll shoot you in the face. Do you understand me? Do you understand? Hey—God himself can't stop me from killing you."

Another time, I went into labor on the Fourth of July. He wanted to go to a party instead. Dropped me at the hospital. Took the boys. By the time they got the contractions under control, he had already started drinking. He came to the wrong hospital, absolutely furious, picked me up and threatened to punch me in the mouth.

We went back to the party. I was in pain. He kept drinking. By the time the fireworks ended, he was too drunk to drive home. I had a horrific migraine and my body was sore from the contractions, but didn't have a choice other than to drive in heavy El Paso traffic. As soon as we were in the car, he started berating me—how stupid and sh*ty and useless I was. How I ruined everything.

I stayed quiet except for asking him to stop so I could focus.

He didn't. He wouldn't.

I reached for my phone to record it. There was absolutely nothing I could say or not say to him to make it stop. He snatched it, yanked the steering wheel, and I lost control of the car for a moment. The kids and I screamed.

We lived on the outskirts of the city and traffic had lightened by then, thank God, but another vehicle—white van—swerved to avoid us. I prayed they would call 911. I prayed for a police checkpoint. Someone radaring on the side of the road I could somehow alert. I thought about driving to the station—but what would I say? It would be my word against his - and he'd already threatened to kill me.

But there was no checkpoint, no radar trap, no hope.

When we pulled into the neighborhood, he told me I'd go missing if I ever talked. That he knew how to make hydrochloric acid. That he'd put me in a blue barrel and no one would find me. That only seven people really cared about me—and they'd stop looking.

> "No one will ever believe you. I'm a respected Green Beret. You're just a birther."

It didn't get better.

By the time our third son was three months old, I often slept on the floor of the guest room with the baby and a gun.

If he ambushed us, he would expect us to be in the bed and I needed a second to react.

Maybe it would give us a chance.

I used to think alcohol was the match.

I didn't know it was gasoline on a fire already out of control.

What We Didn't Know

Drinking has always been a part of military culture. We have evidence of it dating back to the Sumerians, Egyptians, Greeks, and Romans. There's a meme that says something like, "Every culture developed blades, fried dough, and fermentation. It's like humans need to stab something, have a doughnut, and drink a beer."

It's a joke—but it's not wrong.

Alcohol isn't just tolerated in military life—it's ritualized.

Operators don't just drink. They bond, grieve, celebrate, and cope with it. It's there when someone gets promoted, when a baby is born, when a marriage ends. A bottle of good bourbon is a school graduation gift. A cooler of beer waits in the team rooms. A glass is poured out for the fallen.

We shipped it downrange to husbands and friends disguised as brown mouthwash. One of my friends brewed it in a bathtub in Afghanistan. Even in garrison: good day? Have a drink. Bad day? Have two.

And I'm not saying they shouldn't. If anyone deserves a beer, it's our operators.

But over time, I started noticing something.

It wasn't just a coping tool—it was a fuse.

Even the most faithful, grounded, God-honoring men I knew—men who loved their wives and kids—eventually confided they struggled with alcohol at some point in their careers. And every one of them had TBI and PTSD. The trifecta. Always.

That's when I started researching.

What We Didn't Know

- "Posttraumatic stress disorder (PTSD) and substance use disorders (SUD) are prevalent and frequently co-occur... Co-morbid PTSD/SUD is associated with more complex and costly clinical outcomes, including increased physical health problems, poorer social functioning, higher suicide rates, legal issues, increased risk of violence, worse treatment adherence, and less improvement during treatment." (*McCauley et al., Clinical Psychology, 2012)*

- Individuals with PTSD are **2–4 times more likely** than those without to meet criteria for SUD.*(McCauley et al., 2012).*

- Nearly **half (46.4%)** of people with PTSD also meet criteria for substance abuse. *(McCauley et al., 2012; Pietrzak et al., 2011)*

- Among veterans, the more combat exposure they experienced, the more likely they are to misuse alcohol.

- Veterans with high combat exposure had **93% higher odds** of alcohol misuse.Veterans with high combat exposure had 93% higher odds of alcohol misuse *(Burnett-Zeigler et al., 2011).*

- People with PTSD are **14 times more likely** to develop a substance use disorder.(*McCauley, Killeen, Gros, Brady, & Back, 2012, p. 285).*

- Research shows that in individuals with both PTSD and a substance use disorder, hyperarousal and avoidance symptoms are especially severe

(McCauley, Killeen, Gros, Brady, & Back, 2012, p. 286).

- In most cases, **PTSD emerges first, with substance abuse developing later—often as a way to manage the unrelenting symptoms** *(McCauley, Killeen, Gros, Brady, & Back, 2012, p. 286)..*

And yet—no one talks about this with families. Not in pre-deployment briefings. Not in post-deployment reintegration. Not in chaplain offices. Not in command structures. Not much outside of, "Just don't get drunk and get a stripper pregnant."

And certainly not in court.

Alcohol Isn't the Only Drug

The military publicly bans illicit drug use, especially downrange. But the truth? The black market is a part of partner force operations. Operators interact with warlords, militias, and underground networks to obtain intelligence, weapons, vehicles—and drugs are part of the territory.

A former Special Forces soldier told me plainly regarding the members of their partner force:

> "Almost all the guys owned brothels."

Access to drugs—stimulants to stay awake, steroids to boost

performance, recreational use to escape—is often simple, expected, and quietly accepted. The unofficial policy behind the scenes goes something along the lines of: "You're the big boys. Don't let it affect your work, don't get caught, and we'll look the other way."

Teams were given advance notice of drug tests. Command often looked the other way if they were able to. If it didn't mess with the mission, it wasn't discussed.

Does that mean every operator was using? No.

But those who did? They were rarely stopped.

A former operator admitted to resupplying their team medic's inventory with black market drugs to avoid failing audits. One former Special Forces soldier, when asked how many of the guys in his circle used drugs, said:

> "100%. But people weren't in my circle unless they had something to do with the drugs."

There are no published stats on illicit drug use in active-duty Special Operations. But we know it's there. And we know this:

> **Substance use—licit or illicit—makes PTSD and TBI worse. It delays healing, increases aggression, and decreases the success of treatment.** *(Vasterling et al., 2018).*

TBI: The Invisible Saboteur

Traumatic Brain Injury is more than just "getting your bell rung." It affects the endocrine system, the frontal lobe, emotional regulation, decision-making, hormone balance, and impulse control.

A person with TBI:

- Is more likely to face a markedly elevated risk of developing psychiatric challenges—especially depression, anxiety, and irritability—when compared to those without TBI *(Dehbozorgi et al., 2024; Howlett, 2021).*

- Is more likely to turn to substances as a form of self-soothing—or self-medication—to manage lingering emotional, cognitive, and physical distress (Consult UHealth; see UHealth "Substance abuse and traumatic brain injury")

- Who continues to use substances during recovery are formally shown to have slower healing, poorer rehabilitation outcomes, and reduced quality of life compared with those who remain abstinent *(Corrigan et al., 1995; Jorge et al., 2005; E. Xie et al., 2023).*

One meta-analysis found that alcohol use increases

dramatically in the months following TBI—often to cope with insomnia, headaches, and emotional chaos. (*Corrigan et al., 2012)*

But here's the kicker:

> **A traumatic brain injury (TBI) makes the brain more vulnerable to the damaging effects of alcohol and drugs, increasing the risk of cognitive decline, mood instability, and further injury (CDC, 2019).**

A damaged brain doesn't just process substances differently—it spirals faster.

The more they use, the worse the symptoms get. The worse the symptoms, the more they use. It's a loop.

Another study found that alcohol use after TBI leads to a **threefold increase in psychiatric hospitalization** and a **tenfold increase in arrest rates**. (*Bombardier et al., 2002)*

And if endocrine disruption is involved—which it often is in operators—then you're dealing with high cortisol, low testosterone and chronic dysregulation of mood and motivation.

Substance use only worsens this chemical instability. It becomes a trap: chemically, hormonally, behaviorally.

The Trifecta

When PTSD, TBI, and substance use overlap, the outcome is rarely manageable. It's not just an injury or a disorder—it's a collapse. But to the outside world, it looks like:

> "He's just a little pissed off. Drinking too much. Maybe stressed."

What they're really seeing is a man losing control of his neurochemical reality—regardless of whether the world calls him hero or condemns him as a monster.

They don't see the rewired brain.

They don't see the trauma loop.

They don't see the system that trained him to suppress everything and never ask for help.

The Body Count: Sobering Stats

- Alcohol use nearly doubles the likelihood of death by suicide—reflecting a **94% increase in risk** *(Isaacs et al., 2022, as summarized by PHCC, 2024).*

- Research suggests that between **10% and 15% of individuals with alcoholism** die by suicide during their lifetime *(Pompili et al., 2010).*

- Up to **40% of people who die by suicide** have alcohol in their system at the time of death *(SAMHSA, 2016).*

- Between **40% and 63% of intimate partner violence (IPV) incidents** involve alcohol use by the perpetrator, the victim, or both *(Foran & O'Leary, 2008).*

- Alcohol abuse not only increases the likelihood of intimate partner violence (IPV), but also escalates both its **frequency** and **severity** *(Foran & O'Leary, 2008).*

- Children growing up in alcoholic homes face a **two- to threefold increase** in the risk of experiencing emotional, physical, or sexual abuse *(Dube et al., 2001)*

- Veterans with a history of opioid use are **twice as likely** to die by suicide compared to those without such a history *(Bohnert et al., 2011).*

- Among OEF/OIF veterans, those diagnosed with a substance use disorder—particularly when co-occurring with PTSD, TBI, or a mood disorder—had **significantly higher odds** of perpetrating both psychological and physical intimate partner violence (IPV) *(Elbogen et al., 2014).*

Consequences (or Lack Thereof)

When problems surface, the reaction from command is anything but consistent. Jake was ordered to the Army Substance Abuse Program (ASAP) and left saying it simply taught him how to drink without getting caught. A 160th door gunner, reeling from a helicopter crash that killed his friends—one he witnessed firsthand—was charged with DUI, kicked out of the unit, and sent to Korea. Mike was also sent to ASAP, yet remains on active duty with the 160th, appealing for medical retirement despite a courts-martial conviction. As one air operator put it, "That's the difference between being a pilot and being a crew chief."

This isn't just about individual misconduct—it's about leadership failure. Accountability is non-negotiable when service members act out, but discipline must be consistent and immune to rank bias. Anything less erodes trust, undermines readiness, and endangers lives. Leaders who allow destructive behavior to continue without addressing its root causes are complicit in the damage it causes. Real treatment for the underlying injuries that drive substance misuse—most often PTSD or TBI—must be enforced while service members are still in uniform. Without it, the system becomes a loophole culture that quietly condones misconduct, as long as it's not committed by the one wearing the lower rank - and as long as you don't get caught.

The military prides itself on discipline, but discipline without fairness is nothing more than control. When leadership responds to identical misconduct with wildly different consequences based on rank, it sends a clear message: rules are negotiable for some, and absolute for others. This double standard doesn't just fail the individual service members caught in the system—it fails their units, their families, and the mission itself. True readiness demands more than punishing the visible fallout; it requires confronting the hidden wounds that cause it and holding every rank to the same standard of accountability. Until that happens, the cycle will repeat—quietly, predictably, and at the expense of those we claim to protect.

I can't say which night everything finally shifted. But I know the fire had been burning long before I smelled the smoke.

We treat substance use like a personal failure—something a man just needs to "get under control." But this chapter taught me otherwise.

The drinking wasn't the origin of the violence. It was the accelerant.

The real fire was trauma. Untreated injury. Rewired brains. A culture that turned human beings into weapons and sent them home with no plan to rebuild.

I used to pray he would just stop drinking.

Now I pray we stop pretending that's the solution.

Alcohol and drugs don't create abuse or suicidality—they expose it, amplify it, pour gasoline on it.

What was already there became lethal.

There was no version of me that could have saved him.

No perfect wife I could have become that would have made him safe.

I didn't light the match. I didn't mix the chemicals. But I still watched as it burned our lives to the ground.

And I came to the hardest truth of all:

I could not stop what was happening. I could not heal my husband.

If I stayed, one day he would kill me.

God had already sent signs. Mike refused to listen.

And I kept waiting—waiting for God to part the sea for me. But before the waters could divide, I had to trust Him enough to step toward them.

And after years of abuse, I didn't even know what walking looked like. My legs felt paralyzed. My mind doubted itself. My body shook like a frightened animal.

I had nowhere to go.

My family was over a thousand miles away.

My father was gone.

The cavalry wasn't coming.

It was just me, him, and God.

So God did the only thing I would respond to: He removed the ground from beneath my feet.

And then He asked me to walk.

The only other choice was to drown.

"When you pass through the waters, I will be with you; and through the rivers, they shall not overwhelm you." —Isaiah 43:2

Chapter Six: Selected to Fail

Blood Ties

Mike came from a long line of warfighters. A man in his direct family line had served in every major American conflict since the Revolution. It was a badge of honor.

But behind the service was suffering.

Mike and his mother later revealed the abuse they endured from his father—a medically retired Green Beret turned rotary pilot and local hero. A family dog shot in front of the children. Daily fits of rage. Rooms destroyed. A police report that went nowhere because of his father's reputation.

Mike's grandfather, also a veteran, was reportedly so abusive that his sons refused to speak of it—even decades later.

My own family, while largely newer to this country, bore similar scars. I'm the granddaughter of a World War II sniper. The great-granddaughter of a World War I soldier. The niece of more Vietnam vets than I can count.

My father was an incredible man in every way. He grew up without indoor plumbing, put himself through college, and went on to serve in local law enforcement, the Air Force, and later the FBI. He sat on church committees, coached sports, and was the backbone of our family. Yet for all his strength and accomplishments, he was exceedingly emotionally reserved. I used to call him "Stoic the Vast." Raised in a predominantly Swedish family with naval warfare and mercenary roots, stoicism and self-reliance ran deep.

When his own father passed away, Dad, in his early 20's, stepped outside the church because he was tearing up. His uncles followed him out. As he sat down, they stood towering over him, arms crossed. "We are Swedish," they said flatly. "We don't cry."

I once chalked it up to Scandinavian individualism, but now I wonder how much of it was his family's way of coping with trauma—and his own.

My mom was remarkable in her own right. Her father, a World War II sniper, returned home after years in an Italian hospital with a head injury. What followed was heartbreakingly familiar when viewed through the lens of what we now know about trauma and ACE scores. He became a womanizer, abandoned his family for years, and left a trail of total destruction in his wake. Most of his children eventually struggled with substance use disorder. Autoimmune and inflammatory diseases ran rampant. One developed schizophrenia and died by suicide; others lived under the shadow of ideation.

My mom pressed forward—she became a nurse, an advocate for others, and a fierce presence in the lives she touched. But she carried her scars, too: codependence and emotional volatility directly tied to her own health struggles. Truth be told, it's amazing she turned out as well as she did – and that's a credit to her own faith, resilience and mindset.

Looking back, I see the many ways my parents sacrificed and tried to do better than the generations before them. And in many ways, they overwhelmingly did. And while their marriage worked exceedingly well and they balanced each other out, I still grew up between two extremes—caught in the tension of their strengths and their scars, learning early how to balance on that tightrope myself.

And it all lines up to the way we crumbled.

The Selection Process: Who Gets Chosen, and Why?

"One hundred men will test today, but only three will win the Green Beret."— Ballad of the Green Beret

There is no shortage of information on how to become a Green Beret or enter any Special Operations unit. Books, web pages, and social media accounts offer endless advice to hopefuls preparing for the first phase: selection.

To even be considered, a soldier must fall between the ages of 18 and 36, hold at least the rank of E-3, and have no more than 14 years of service. They must qualify for a secret clearance, score at least 110 on the technical ASVAB, and be eligible to serve a minimum of 36 months post-training.

Candidates often train for months—sometimes years—for SFAS (Special Forces Assessment and Selection), a grueling physical and psychological crucible. Over several weeks, hundreds of men complete physical fitness tests, land navigation, team-building exercises, rucks, swims in boots and gear, obstacle courses—all while under constant scrutiny. Roughly 36% of candidates are selected to move forward to the Special Forces Qualification Course (SFQC). Of those, about 80% will go on to graduate.

While the emphasis is often on physical performance, psychological screening plays a crucial role. How do they solve problems? How do they interact with teammates? Do they lead or fracture the group? Can they perform under pressure? They specifically look for resilience, which is essentially measured by how quickly a candidate "gets back up and in the game" after a setback or failure.

Selected candidates tend to score higher in neuroticism and narcissism than the general population. These traits, in moderation, can be protective in combat. The ability to suppress emotion, maintain control under fire, and dissociate from moral injury is what keeps teams alive. They display increased confidence, emotional compartmentalization, and a capacity to act without empathy—traits necessary to remain composed and lethal in catastrophic conditions.

These aren't necessarily indicators of a personality disorder, but they do map closely onto diagnostic criteria when pushed to extremes under prolonged stress. And when amplified by combat and training, they often morph into maladaptive behaviors.

According to legend, my father spent an early part of his FBI career helping develop the Bureau's psychological profiling program and wrote its first official training manual on how to conduct interrogations. I can attest to his ability to read people — even my own friends — and tell me things about them I didn't yet know but that always proved to be spot-on. He could do it just from the way they walked into a room and spoke.

When he met Mike, he used one of the oldest tricks in the book: he got him drunk, letting him believe they were going toe-to-toe in a friendly drinking match, while quietly holding back, making conversation while watching and measuring.

The next morning, he half-laughed, smiled broadly, and told me Mike was a good guy — just to watch the drinking, because "he can really put them back."

Maybe my father missed something. Or maybe there was nothing to miss yet. Either way, Mike cleared the kind of expert-level vetting that most people will never experience — and he still went on to become dangerous.

That's the uncomfortable truth: you can't always see what war will make of a man. And if a seasoned profiler can be fooled by what isn't there yet, how much more easily can our military screening processes be fooled?

Some of the best humans I know are operators. But many? If they didn't suffer from something before, they probably do now.

The screenings attempt to weed out men with extreme psychopathic or narcissistic traits. But ironically, the very skills that help them succeed—emotional detachment, manipulation, charm—also make them harder to detect during evaluations. Many are masterful at masking.

I still believe most operators are sheepdogs, but it would be naïve to ignore the wolves lurking among them.

Unseen Costs: Trauma Recruits Trauma

The deeper issue isn't the selection process itself—it's the pool from which the candidates come.

Childhood trauma is a silent recruiter. Kids exposed to abuse, neglect, addiction, or chaos develop coping mechanisms that meld and forge exactly the kind of adults Special Operations seeks: high-performing, hyper-vigilant, and mission-focused with the ability to hyper-compartmentalize. Adverse Childhood Experiences (ACEs), like volatile home environments, become a breeding ground for elite warriors.

And it works—at first.

But data shows that those same high ACE scores predict devastating outcomes later in life. Soldiers with traumatic childhoods are far more likely to develop severe PTSD symptoms if they experience combat trauma. They also face higher risks for substance abuse, chronic illness, and relational instability. The very traits that make them successful in war often destroy a home environment.

And the military isn't telling them—or their families—that.

Out of the many operators I've spoken to in-depth, only one had an ACE score below six. All had dealt with suicidal ideation, regardless. All admitted to painting a rosier picture of their upbringing during evaluations.

One operator told me, "We all had PTSD before we had PTSD. Something's got to be off for anyone to volunteer for a job guaranteed to make it worse."

Of course, not every man in Special Operations fits this profile. There are always exceptions. But data doesn't lie—many, if not most, do. And that matters.

Built to Serve, Broken by Silence

"41% of military officers come from military families." *(Bryant & Swaney, Deconstructing the Warrior Caste)*

"78% of servicemembers hail from families of generational service."

Blue Star Families reported in 2016 that 45% of active duty, 47% of military spouses, and 57% of veteran respondents had a parent who served.

Over 53% of respondents had two or more immediate family members who served.

A son whose father served is five times more likely to join the military.

This is what researchers call professional inheritance—a pattern where children follow parents into career paths they're familiar with. But what happens when those careers carry psychological damage that's never treated?

PTSD wasn't recognized as a clinical diagnosis until 1980. Veterans from WWII, Vietnam, Korea—most had no access to mental health support. Instead, they brought their war wounds home, disguised as silence, rage, alcoholism, or detachment. Their children—a great portion of the GWOT generation—grew up in those environments.

And research is clear:

- Children exposed to parents with PTSD are **significantly more likely** to develop severe PTSD symptoms themselves (Napolitano, 2015).

- Adverse Childhood Experience (ACE) scores are predictive of both PTSD vulnerability and symptom severity, even when controlling for combat exposure (Magos & Rosas, 2019).

- Even healthy adults with high ACE scores are **360% more likely** to develop heart disease, and those with a score of six or more face **up to 20 years' reduction in lifespan** (Felitti et al., 1998).

This isn't just about the individual soldier. It's about what happens when war becomes generational. Research shows that trauma compounds across generations. It's not just passed down—it multiplies.

Today's operators are more likely to come from warrior families. More likely to have grown up around untreated PTSD. More likely to score high on ACE questionnaires. More likely to develop PTSD themselves—and suffer more intensely when they do.

And yet, despite this knowledge, military policy hasn't caught up. Support systems are underfunded or inaccessible. Psychological screenings don't account for compounded trauma. Families are left in the dark, wondering why their war hero is now unpredictable, violent, or emotionally unavailable.

This is especially true for military spouses. The likelihood of a woman marrying a service member increases dramatically if her father also served. Many were raised with similar values—service, sacrifice, silence. When abuse enters the home, they struggle to seek help. Not just out of fear, but out of loyalty. Out of belief that this is the cost of duty.

But it isn't.

We are selecting these men—consciously or not—from the children who were hurt the worst, forging them into warriors by building on broken foundations. And we're doing it without warning them, without treating them, and without giving their families the tools to survive it.

They are largely selected to fail—because their wounds are invisible until it's too late—and the system often gaslights the literal life out of them when they do.

The Consequences: A National Security Crisis in the Making

The question has been asked in newsrooms, op-eds, VA hospitals, and around kitchen tables: Why is this generation suffering so severely from "PTSD?"

Some point to the relentless operational tempo of the Global War on Terror (GWOT)—multiple combat deployments, extended tours, and the rise of asymmetrical warfare. Others have hypothesized that the long boat rides home allowed men to decompress before reuniting with their families.

But it doesn't tell the whole story.

What we're witnessing is not just the psychological cost of modern combat or the deadly trifecta. It's the compounded interest of unhealed generational trauma.

And if 78% of our fighting force comes from families of generational service, the future of our country's ability to protect itself looks grim.

We're losing 22–44 soldiers a day to suicide. 90% of Special Forces marriages end in divorce. Over a quarter of military kids surveyed in California—not a state known for its combat-specific units—report experiencing suicidal ideation.

We are breeding warriors in war zones at home—and calling it honor.

If we don't acknowledge and address this cycle now—not later, not politically, not performatively—now—the future of our military readiness and national security is at serious risk.

And in the meantime, we will continue to lose some of our best minds, our strongest bodies, and our most loyal patriots—not to the battlefield, but to what happens when they come home.

This isn't just a mental health crisis.

It's a national security one.

It's hard to speak out against the people, places, and systems we've spent so long protecting—especially when we love them. When they've shaped us. When they've become part of our very identity.

Moses must have known that feeling. He had been raised by the very Pharaoh he would one day confront. Egypt wasn't just the land of Israel's slavery—it was also the place where Moses was

clothed, fed, and given a name. To confront it meant confronting part of his own story.

And Egypt wasn't all whips and chains. The people grew comfortable there. Enslaved, yes—but they knew what the next day would bring. They knew they would have food. It was their home. They had lived there for four hundred years—longer than our country has even existed. It was the devil they knew.

Later in the wilderness, when they grew tired of manna and the future uncertain, they even longed to go back. That's how silence works, too. It promises safety in familiarity. It whispers: At least you know how this goes. At least you can predict the pain.

Speaking up feels like stepping into the unknown. But God doesn't leave His people in Egypt. He calls us out, even when it's terrifying, even when it feels like betrayal of everything we've known. Because silence is not safety—it's slavery. And His promise is not survival in captivity. It's freedom.

I had my own Egypt. The day I chose to break silence—to call the police, to file the report, to tell the truth—I felt like I was stepping into a wilderness with no map. I didn't know if I would survive it. In fact, Mike had promised that I wouldn't. And the fear still lingers. But my faith

has grown because I finally let God show up—parting seas I thought were impossible, sending manna each morning when the last day's reserves had run out. And He did.

The day I made that call, the day I started writing, the day I chose to testify—I knew the truth might cost me everything. I might die in the wilderness. In fact, Mike promised that I would. But at least I would die free.

And when words failed me, I found comfort in the prayer of Thomas Merton, who captured the wilderness walk of faith better than I ever could:

> *"My Lord God, I have no idea where I am going. I do not see the road ahead of me. I cannot know for certain where it will end. Nor do I really know myself, and the fact that I think I am following Your will does not mean that I am actually doing so. But I believe that the desire to please You does in fact please You. And I hope I have that desire in all that I am doing. I hope that I will never do anything apart from that desire. And I know that, if I do this, You will lead me by the right road, though I may know nothing about it. Therefore I will trust You always though I may seem to be lost and in the shadow of death. I will not fear, for You are ever with me, and You will never leave me to face my perils alone. Amen."*

If you're still in Egypt—still stuck in silence, still afraid of what happens if you speak—I want you to know this: God will not leave you there. He is already calling you out.

Freedom is terrifying. It is dangerous. It comes with unknowns and heartbreaks. But it is also the only place where real hope and truthfaith begin.

> *"Do not be afraid. Stand firm and you will see the deliverance the Lord will bring you today... The Lord will fight for you; you need only to be still." -Exodus 14:13–14*

Chapter Seven: Reality vs Reporting

"If all Special Operations soldiers were completely transparent regarding their mental health status and the current response policies were applied in every single case, the United States Military would be unable to sustain its operational capabilities."

I shared this statement with a group of operators and their families and asked, "Agree or disagree?"

I was expecting some pushback, but the response was unanimous: this statement was met with *complete and unilateral* agreement. A seasoned operator even took it a step further—expanding the statement to include support staff as well.

Special Operations service members supposedly have the highest access to both mental and physical health care - far and above what "conventional" units have access to, though. So why aren't they getting it? Even friends who work in SOF schools noted that, "The resources are there." But are they?

The answer is yes—and overwhelmingly, no.

The Truth Behind the Numbers

The numbers don't match reality for a reason.

This chapter isn't about the symptoms—it's about why they aren't being treated. Why soldiers hide them. Why commands minimizes them. Why spouses whisper about them instead of scream.

Because if the military acknowledged how widespread these problems are—if it told the truth about the sheer number of operators struggling with PTSD, TBI, and addiction—the entire system would collapse under the weight of accountability. So instead, it silences them. And until now, we've let it happen under the false banner of strength and service—a polished tarp thrown over very real suffering.

Prevalence estimates by the VA suggest only 11–18% of soldiers who have seen combat are reported to experience PTSD. The numbers don't reflect what we see in our communities, and there are many reasons why.

First and foremost: soldiers suffering from combat-related mental health issues are discouraged—directly or indirectly—from reporting or seeking care. This deterrent stems from lack of access, ineffective treatments, and a culture of fear built through years of punitive policy, and a culturally ingrained idea that the admission of humanity *is* failure.

An active-duty Special Forces officer called me nearly in tears. One of his men, also a SF combat veteran, had reached a breaking point. Operators are inherently tough—quietly, unassumingly. Admitting injury or "complaining" is not part of their wiring. When an operator asks for help, it's generally assumed as being incredibly critical.

The officer immediately reached out to and left a voicemail

with the battalion psychiatrist. Two days passed—no response. He followed up with another call, an email, and a text. Still nothing.

Several days later, the psychiatrist finally responded: the next available appointment—anywhere the soldier was authorized to seek care—was six weeks out.

Another operator with a severe TBI was told to "swaddle himself like a baby, confine himself to a closet, and stare at a lava lamp."

One servicemember —who had never used illegal drugs—was labeled an addict by his behavioral health care provider. The provider made conflicting statements about his behavior and willingness to seek treatment, which not only jeopardized his access to appropriate care but also put him at risk of being discharged for something he didn't do at all. The office staff made this same servicemember aware that he was **not** the only patient who faced this issue and they hoped that it would finally be addressed.

From conversations with dozens of active-duty and retired operators, it's also clear that behavioral health care providers often underdiagnose and prescribe the lowest level of treatment possible:

a. To release the military and themselves from liability if the soldier spirals

b. To keep the soldier deployable (more on that

shortly.)

Multiple operators told me their behavioral health provider explicitly stated what *not* to say during sessions—advice that helped protect their careers, but ultimately kept them from receiving the care they truly needed. And behavioral health providers in the military often walk a fine line: trying to build enough trust to understand what their patients are actually facing so they can attempt to treat them effectively, while also protecting those patients from career-ending disclosures. In doing so, they sometimes end up protecting the system more than the soldier.

Soldiers report that the "psychs throw pills at us and hope the problems go away."

One Special Operations aviator told me, "They said I was fine—they were full of sh*t. Their job is to keep us on flight status." The same soldier, struggling with explosive anger, was told to put an ice pack on his neck when he felt upset.

The Culture of Fear

Even those willing to seek help can face long waits. Clinics are frequently understaffed with a high turnover rate. Behavioral health providers rotate in and out. Continuity of care suffers - which actually lowers treatment efficacy rates.

And fear is ever-present.

A study found that in 2009, there was a sudden and continued spike in discharges related to soldiers who reported PTSD-like symptoms. Trouble at home became a dangerous secret—shared only with the most trusted. And while I can say from personal experience that the culture has improved somewhat and mental health is now discussed more openly, cultural progress hasn't translated into meaningful policy reform. The fear remains. Multiple operators disclosed that they would not seek help until their careers were effectively over, for fear of being taken out of the game and forced to medically retire early - or worse.

The official line says there are no consequences for seeking help. The reality? Reporting symptoms often feels like playing Russian roulette with your career. A service member's access to care largely depends on command support—or lack thereof—and often hinges on their personal relationship with their commander. If you're on good terms, you're probably safe. If you've butted heads, reporting can become a convenient excuse to push you out.

One operator nearly lost his career after a family member reported a suicidal episode. He and his family denied it, called it exaggerated, and the matter was quietly dropped. This isn't rare. Almost all of soldiers I've spoken with have struggled with suicidal ideation but remain high-functioning at work.

And they know better than to report it.

Newer soldiers learn fast. One operator just entering his unit told me bluntly he would never report any issue—mental or physical—for fear of jeopardizing his career and his family's financial security.

What we're really looking at are two terrible options our servicemembers face:

1. Stay quiet, keep their job, and hope they don't implode before retirement.

2. Speak up, gamble on leadership, risk their career, and land in the VA system.

But that's not a choice. It's a rigged game.

The Malinois Mentality

Most choose silence. Most minimize. "If a guy has any team time left," one operator told me, "he'll do everything he can to stay on the team."

It's a sentiment I've heard from nearly every operator I've ever spoken with: an ingrained desire to do what they were trained to do—what they believe they were *made* to do.

Most military working dogs are Belgian Malinois—fierce, undeterred, and relentless in completing their objectives. Even when seriously injured, they press on until the job is done, sometimes collapsing only afterward. Their handlers have to watch for subtle signs in the middle of chaos, because the dog will not stop on its own.

Operators are much more than dogs, but the comparison holds. The drive to finish the mission isn't just cultural—it's physiological, mental, and spiritual. Years of training and repetition have wired them to override pain, suppress fear, and ignore the body's warning signs. Stopping feels like betrayal—not only to the mission, but to their teammates, their identity, and everything they've sacrificed to get there.

Telling an operator—who has spent years conditioning every fiber of his being for war—to sit out is like telling a Malinois to stay in the kennel while the fight happens right outside. It's not just frustrating—it's alien. It's against everything they've prepared to become and do. Rest and recovery feel inexplicably wrong, even dangerous, when they know their brothers are stepping into harm's way without them.

And so, they press on—through headaches that blur their vision, through rages they don't understand, and through pain that would sideline most professional athletes. They keep going until the mission is over, even if it means collapsing—sometimes literally—the moment the dust settles.

Because in their world, the worst wound isn't physical injury. It's being left behind.

And that mindset also impacts reporting. It's why multiple operators I interviewed admitted they only sought care once an injury had already ended their careers—when there was nothing left to lose, and when staying in the fight was no longer an option. By then, the damage to their bodies and brains was at least partially irreversible, and any hope of earlier intervention had long passed.

No Data? No Problem to Solve.

And the data we do have? It's broken.

Diagnostic criteria vary. Most studies rely on self-reporting. Many involve veterans already in the VA. No consistent, official mental health survey exists for active-duty combat soldiers that's taken at regular screening intervals post-combat.

So why doesn't leadership want better data?

Because it threatens everything.

Funding. Operational tempo. Readiness stats. Deployable numbers.

OPTEMPO and OPRED—the measures of how often soldiers deploy and whether units are mission-ready—are the lifeblood of force projection.

Like a retail store needing a minimum number of employees, the military needs a minimum number of operators to function. But operators are scarce. Only 1% of Americans serve. Just 5% of those fall under Special Operations. Of that, only a fraction are actual operators - yet they conduct over 90% of battlefield missions.

They understaffed and massively overworked.

This leads to:

- Providers underdiagnosing.
- Soldiers suppressing symptoms.
- Crushing guilt when stepping down.
- And a higher rate of training accident fatalities - especially in aviation.

One soldier said, "If I leave, there's no one else. I'd be abandoning my unit—and my country."

That's not resilience. That's desperation.

And with broken data, there's no crisis to acknowledge—no responsibility to take.

I asked a couple of young operators if there was anywhere or anyone they could talk to about what they were facing without potentially triggering career-ending consequences. "The chaplain," they both echoed.

That's it. The chaplain.

And chaplains are often overworked and understaffed. A single chaplain might serve anywhere from **500 to 1,500 soldiers—and their families**. They also vary widely in training. One might have a master's in social work and be fluent in family dynamics and trauma-informed care. Others? Not so much.

I reached out to a chaplain during my first marriage. Jake was already becoming verbally abusive before he even came home. He'd accuse me of cheating on him while I was asleep beside my computer and phone—waiting weeks sometimes between his calls, which often descended into chaos. His best friend wasn't even allowed in our house unless another woman was present. I didn't go out and party - just worked and went to the barn and waited for his calls.

I didn't understand what was happening or where this was coming from and was desperate for guidance.

The chaplain told me not to worry about my husband's behavior—then asked if I knew it was biblically acceptable to fantasize about him when I was alone.

A Cracking Mirror

Add it up: TBI-related impulsivity, PTSD-related aggression, SUD-driven disinhibition. Compartmentalized empathy. Higher-than-average scores in narcissism and neuroticism. Childhood trauma layered beneath it all. A system that punishes people for seeking help that they desperately need and on the most basic levels of human decency - deserve? It's no wonder why they crumble as soon as they step through the threshold into their homes. Who wouldn't? And cost - hits families hard, too. SOF has an estimated 90% divorce rate. I'm not saying that all wives are angels and not causative, but when you have that level of pressure on our men and their families - there are going to be major cracks.

And while you can now understand how and why domestic violence happens in our families, it's not accepted in Special Operations culture. When wives are able to successfully document abuse, the response is often swift and brutal: "Lock him up." "Strip the Beret." "Kick him out."

When I shared our story with trusted operators, most responded with horror, empathy, even offers of protection.

DV and IPV violate the SF creed: "I will not bring shame upon myself or Special Forces." But demonizing these men doesn't fix the problem. It hardens it. Shame builds walls—around perpetrators and victims alike.

I watched my husband swing between shame and denial. Special Operations ingrained in men the idea that they are elite. Invincible. Or should be. They perform near-impossible missions, afterall. When they fail at home, they don't just disappoint themselves—they betray a myth.

When abuse happens, they have two options:

- Shatter the myth and risk emotional collapse.
- Deflect blame to preserve the image.

"She's crazy."

"She started it."

"I wasn't like this until I married you."

No—you weren't like this until you came home from war.

A friend once asked, "If these guys are so out of control, why don't they hit their commanders? Why only their wives and kids?"

I sat with that and greatly struggled with her words before reaching out to an operator who had been accused of domestic violence. He made an interesting hypothesis and it had to do with moral injury, self loathing, and proximity. Combat certainly takes its toll and many, if not most, of our operators suffer from some elements of operator syndrome. When the perceived failure of OEF and OIF, the retaking of Afghanistan by the Taliban, difficulty reintegrating to life stateside when they are fabled to be unstoppable, and the obstacles they face to maintain personal relationships as well as their on mental health are added to the equation, many may feel inadequate to the point of self-loathing. If it's true that family members are often perceived, whether correctly or incorrectly, as an extension of oneself, they become the nearest target for that anger and frustration. It doesn't make it right, but I think that process, or something similar to it, occurs in at least some of the cases.

Insecurity is often a hallmark of narcissistic behavior and arrogance is frequently a form of overcompensation for imposter syndrome or, at a minimum, insecurity. When they come home from war and all is not perfect, or when those closest to them see their imperfections as opposed to the persona they attempt to project and believe they are expected to uphold in every area of their lives, tension is immediately amplified and the reaction may include implosion.

But the Department of Defense isn't tracking that.
According to *Military.com*, *"The Defense Department recorded more than 42,000 incidents of domestic abuse in its population from 2015 to 2019—but the real number is likely higher. That's because the data collected by the department is incomplete, according to a new report from the Government Accountability Office.*
By law, *the DoD must collect and report data on incidents that meet its criteria for domestic abuse. But it fails to consistently collect information on all allegations and fails to substantiate many complaints, making it difficult for the Pentagon to understand the scope of the problem,* ***GAO auditors told Congress*** *in a report released earlier this month."*

"By law."

The DoD is breaking it.

Congress was informed.

<u>The Gag Order: Family Reporting Systems</u>

If domestic violence or concerning behavior occurs at home, spouses have four options - and all are incredibly problematic.

When domestic violence or concerning behavior occurs at home, military spouses have three options—and all three are problematic.
First, they can contact commands. In the military, a servicemember's command is nearly godlike in power. They can involve CID, institute formal punishments like pay forfeiture or a permanently filed GOMOR (a potential career-ender), reassign the soldier, mandate counseling—or they can sweep it under the rug.

In my experience—and in the accounts of countless victims and victim advocates —command tends to protect the soldier, no matter how serious the accusation. This is especially true in Special Operations.

Why? Because these soldiers are expensive to replace. Their training is specialized, lengthy, and costly. The military invests years—and often millions of dollars—into each operator. And when staffing shortages are already a chronic issue, leadership often prioritizes force readiness over family safety.

Then the family is left with a service member who now knows two things: that his behavior was reported—and that there will be no consequences.

What follows is often rage. Retaliation. A new level of danger.

Because in his mind, she broke the unspoken rule—she exposed him.

The second option is to file a report with Family Advocacy. There are two types: **restricted** and **unrestricted**.

A **restricted report** is based on minimal information. Essentially: *"We have a problem at home."* It allows spouses to access resources like counseling and classes, but it comes with no consequences for the service member. No investigation. No command notification. No one requiring him to get help—or be held accountable.
That's because restricted reports are intentionally vague, leaving little more than a vague paper trail.

After the gun incident, I chose to file a restricted report—to at least leave that trail.

So did Megan Santiago, the wife of a SOF support soldier. She filed a restricted report, too—**right before she was killed.**

But the same fate can await the women who file those reports. Their allegations can still be ignored, minimized, or buried.

The same risk exists with the **fourth reporting option**: contacting civilian police.

In both cases, abusers often respond with counteraccusations—claiming the spouse is unstable, abusive, or manipulative. These claims are rarely backed by evidence, but that doesn't stop them from being used in court to discredit the victim.

Even baseless accusations can sway a judge or commander—especially in a system designed to protect **the myth under the uniform**.

Retaliation

Victims don't just face threats from their abuser—they can also face retaliation from those close to him (Institute for Women's Policy Research 2020; Bellotti, Paolucci, and Zaccaria 2021). Mike once told me that if he couldn't kill me himself, his team or someone his family knew would.
Years earlier, when his affair partner reached out to me, Mike showed me a text from one of the guys offering to help "take care of her." It made me realize how easily he could spin a story, paint me as the problem, and have me "taken care of," too. Even among our mutual friends, I wasn't sure who I could trust.

Not long after his arrest, my youngest son woke up in the middle of the night crying. I was in his room, trying to soothe him, when the heavy thrum of rotor blades ripped through the quiet. A helicopter dropped low over our roof, shaking the house. I laid over my son and froze. I didn't know if Mike had somehow gotten hold of a bird and was about to end his life by ending ours, if one of his guys was sending a message, or if it was simply meant to terrify us into silence.

Later, when we were considering reconciliation, Mike insisted it wasn't him—but admitted he knew who it was. That was all the confirmation I needed. It wasn't random. Even with protective orders in place, we weren't safe—not from him, and not from the people who stood with him.

I didn't report it. By then I was juggling court hearings, business obligations, and caring for my children—while still trying to process years of trauma and keep the world from collapsing on us. And what was I going to do? I didn't know who was flying—but at the time I was pretty sure it was Mike, or someone he knew. Reporting it would mean putting myself in the position of having to confront the very people who might have carried it out—or worse, authorized it.
And that's what the system never seems to understand: when the burden falls on victims to document and report every threat, every act of intimidation, silence is not consent—it's survival.

And whoever flew that helicopter—they're still out there.

On The Record

Before we close this chapter, I want to put a few things on the record.

Not every operator is an abuser. These are still some of the best our country has to offer—by and far.

In fact, considering the data and the risk factors, the reality that this *isn't* happening in every family is a borderline miracle—**a testament to the caliber of men staffing these units.**

But that doesn't mean that these men aren't suffering - even if they aren't hurting their families.

And that doesn't mean abuse isn't happening—likely at two to three times the rate currently reported.

Not every wife is a saint. Some women are damaged. Some do make false accusations. And yes, false reports exist—and those women should face accountability under the law, too.

That's exactly why we need a system that can tell the difference.

A system that protects the innocent, holds the guilty accountable, and doesn't punish victims for coming forward or service members who seek care BEFORE it hits the fan.

The current system is failing at all of that. Massively.
And the data shows it's doing so *intentionally*.

Moses didn't set out to be a prophet or a liberator. He was a fugitive—running from failure, hiding in

the desert, content to live far away from the cries of his people. He built a new life, a new home. He wasn't planning on going back.

But then God showed up in fire. A bush that burned and was not consumed. If we're being honest here, Moses probably thought he gathered the wrong kind of mushrooms. And when the call came, Moses resisted: "Pardon your servant, Lord. I have never been eloquent... I am slow of speech and tongue" (Exodus 4:10).

He knew he wasn't enough. He was just one man, with a stammer, standing against the most powerful empire on earth.

That's how it feels to speak against the military machine. One voice against a system that would rather you stay quiet. Reports buried. Data suppressed. Service members and families gagged by fear and policy. It's Pharaoh all over again—armies, decrees, power used to keep truth in chains. And like Moses, it's easy to think: "Who am I to speak?"

I've felt that. I resisted. I even quit writing altogether for a time. I ran from this book more times than I can count. There are still days when I want to pack up my kids, start over somewhere far away, and pretend none of this ever happened—or

is still happening.

But God's answer to Moses wasn't to boost his confidence. It was to remind him of who goes with him: "Who gave human beings their mouths? ... Now go; I will help you speak and will teach you what to say" (Exodus 4:11–12).

Moses went back to confront the very Pharaoh who had once wanted him dead. And in my own way, I've had to do the same. To go back—not just to the memories, but to the system, the courts, the machine that threatened to destroy me—and speak. Not because I am strong, but because God has commanded me to open my mouth.

Moses didn't free Israel because he was eloquent or brave. He freed them because God spoke through him. One trembling man with a speech impediment became the mouthpiece of heaven, and Pharaoh's gag orders crumbled in the face of God's command: "Let my people go."

That's the hope for us too. We don't need perfect words. We don't need power, or rank, or permission. We need only obedience. To speak when God says speak. To trust that our weakness doesn't disqualify us—it becomes the very place His strength shows through.

So yes, one voice can matter. One voice can break gag orders. Not just mine - but yours too. Because it is not really ours. It is His. And if He calls us to speak, then silence is no longer an option.
"His word is in my heart like a fire, a fire shut up in my bones. I am weary of holding it in; indeed, I cannot" - Jeremiah 20:9.

Chapter Eight: The War We Can't Win

As the years passed, I started to notice something about the other wives I'd stayed in touch with—everyone was getting sick.

Cancer scares. Autoimmune diseases. Chronic pain.

Almost all of us were dealing with anxiety, sleep problems, or some form of depression. A few had wrestled with suicidal thoughts. One team wife had to ask a friend to come take the guns out of her house after she found out her husband was having an affair. She didn't trust herself not to do something permanent.

None of us had been to war. But all of us were carrying it.

The sleep deprivation. The solo parenting. The unspoken expectation to absorb every reintegration, deployment, and move without complaint. The pressure to smile through it so their mission could stay on track.

It wears on you—even in good marriages.

And the truth is: whether or not abuse occurs—whether a spouse stays or leaves—there are long-term physical, psychological, and financial consequences for women exposed to combat from the sidelines.

In The Blast Radius

These are the hidden casualties of war—the ones not

counted in any deployment report or readiness assessment.

- **Mental Health:** Partners of veterans with PTSD are significantly more likely to experience anxiety, depression, and symptoms of secondary traumatic stress (Dekel & Monson, 2010).

- **Suicide Risk:** Spouses of service members were **47% more likely** to die by suicide than civilian peers of the same sex and age bracket (Department of Defense, 2019; CDC, 2019). Women who were victims of intimate partner violence (IPV) in higher-risk categories were **2.7–3.8 times** more likely to die by suicide than those in lower-risk categories, and **1 in 5** IPV survivors threatened or attempted suicide in their lifetime (Campbell et al., 2003).

- **Physical Health:** Chronic stress impairs immune function. Many spouses develop autoimmune disorders, cardiovascular issues, hormonal dysregulation, and persistent fatigue (Boscarino, 2008; Yehuda et al., 2005).

- **Career + Identity Loss:** Frequent moves, solo parenting, and unpredictable schedules don't just disrupt careers—they erode identity. Women who were once confident, ambitious, creative... begin to disappear into the shadow of the mission.

- **Financial Instability:** Whether they stay or leave,

> many spouses end up in financial free fall. Divorce doesn't guarantee safety—or solvency. Most walk away with less than they brought in, are forced to start over from scratch with no career experience, and re-build with a much later start - which often leads to financial stress and even greater impact on mental and physical health. Those who stay often forfeit their own earning potential trying to hold the family together.

Spouses don't just support the warfighter. They absorb the war. And there are enough studies to back this up to warrant its own book. (If you're interested in reading one already written, check out Stacy Bannerman's work, "Homefront 9/11.")

And while conventional units may no longer be "in the fight," Special Operations service members remain active. They're still out there—on high-risk hostage rescue missions and quietly engaging enemies in the shadows around the world. For them, the war may never be over. And for their spouses, neither will its cost.

The Silence Within

Special Operations families tend to be more stable, at least geographically. But that stability comes at a cost.

Everyone is dealing with some version of the same thing at home. Maybe not outright abuse, but always some level of suffering: emotional volatility. Disconnection. Suicidality.

Substance misuse. Wives running on fumes.

And because we see it all around us—because the families next door are still "holding it together"—we internalize the message:

"We're all in the suck. So who are you to complain?"

If your kids go to school together, if your husbands deploy together—you know that speaking out won't just affect your home. It might take your husband offline. That could compromise the team's readiness. Which could endanger your friend's husband—and their children's father.

So you weigh it: His career. Their mission. Your silence.

The system, whether intentional or not, is built to make leaving feel like betrayal.

The War At Home

But when abuse does happen—when the very person they've built their life around becomes the source of danger—that invisible labor becomes a war zone of its own.

And when they choose to leave, the consequences to the victim are swift and often severe. We've already discussed the lack of safe reporting options for military spouses. But that's only one thread in a much larger web. Finances, cultural dynamics, systemic silence, and legal inconsistencies all conspire to keep victims caught - and then effectively punish them when they do come forward.

Financial Entrapment

Most military families rely on a single income—the service member's. Side hustles rarely generate enough for spouses to live independently, let alone cover childcare or legal representation. Over the years, legal fees alone consumed 20–30% of my pre-tax income.

Even therapy was out of reach. Twelve weeks of in-person sessions would've required babysitters, gas, and time I didn't have. The commute and babysitting alone would've cost over $1,000.

It makes sense when you zoom out. Frequent moves disrupt employment and sever support networks. Many military spouses are left juggling childcare, home management, and the emotional fallout experienced by their children as a result of their partner's unpredictable schedule. Building a stable career in that chaos is hard. Keeping one is harder.

For lower-enlisted families, the barriers are even steeper: one car. One income. No nearby family.

I've lost count of how many women I've heard crying for help—trapped in their homes with no transportation, no support system, no family within hundreds of miles... and no way out except a hotel room they probably can't afford. If they can get out at all.

"What About Shelters?"

That's not much of an option either.

- The only shelter in our area that had space wouldn't accept male children.
- There are no domestic violence shelters on post—no emergency quarters set aside for spouses and their children in crisis.

If you want help, you have to call the police, file an unrestricted report through FAP, or notify your partner's command. And even then, the command decides whether to remove the service member from the home. That decision is often tied to administrative or punitive action—which means the spouse isn't just asking for help. She's triggering a process that could potentially end her partner's career.

She knows what that means.

When I reported, he drained our joint bank accounts. He claimed our children on his tax return—even though he hadn't seen them in nearly a year. It cost me almost $10,000. My lawyer shrugged.

> "There's nothing we can do."

The Legal Gamble

The justice system has no consistent playbook for abuse survivors—especially when the abuser is a service member.

Cultural attitudes can be supportive... or devastating.

One attorney told me I sounded like a bitter woman trying to ruin my husband. Another said I wasn't angry enough to be believed. They all asked the same thing:

> "If it was really that bad, how could you possibly have stayed so long?"

Many service members dismissed the idea that a domestic violence problem exists. One referred to it as "home problems."

I chalk that up to the fact that they couldn't imagine behaving that way themselves. Which, frankly, is a good thing. But what they don't realize is that **the home is the canary in the coal mine**. That's the first place soldiers begin to unravel,and the first people to witness that unraveling are their families.

It didn't matter how much evidence I had. How calm I was. How angry I was. How carefully I documented everything. Someone always had something to say—about what I should have done, or who they thought I was.

As if surviving abuse—and daring to seek safety—automatically made me suspicious.

This isn't just my story. It's a national pattern.

- A 2015 survey by the National Domestic Violence

Hotline found that **58% of survivors who sought help felt the system made things worse**.

- Researcher Alesha Durfee (2011) wrote: *"Women who report abuse are often met with skepticism—especially when their abuser is perceived as respectable or holds a position of authority."

Maybe Mike was right. He was a Green Beret. And I was just a birther. He had the image. I had the evidence.

Guess which one the jury believed.

Local police were courageous, compassionate, and trauma-informed. But CID was a different story.

The first agent I spoke to—a woman who'd graduated from the same law enforcement training as I had—looked me in the eye and said:

> "Do you really want to ruin his career? There must still be some love there... you have three kids together."

As if I hadn't spent eight years quietly holding it together. As if I hadn't become a shell of a person in the process.

She recused herself.

The second agent had over 25 years of experience in domestic violence. He was compassionate and determined. After hearing the full scope, he told a family member:

> "This ends here." And then, gently: "She'll probably never be okay again after what Mike did to her."

But as we prepared for the court-martial, we discovered that a critical audio recording—captured minutes before the gun incident—was missing from the evidence provided to the prosecution.

When I told a JAG staff member, they didn't deflect:

> "I'm not surprised. It happens all the time."

And still, the question remains:

Will I be believed?

Studies show that women from lower-income backgrounds are often seen as unstable or complicit, while those from higher socioeconomic status—or considered attractive—are viewed as manipulative or calculating (Moran, 2021; Epstein & Goodman, 2018; Dion et al., 1972).

There is no "right" kind of victim. Just a courtroom shaped by bias.

Judges are human. Research confirms that judicial decisions in family violence cases vary widely—even when the facts are identical (Meier, 2016).

I had a bruise from the gun barrel—an "O" pattern clearly visible. I had audio recordings where he admitted to drinking whiskey that day.

But it didn't matter. I was accused of provoking him—of trying to "trap" him.

There were so many incidents I couldn't document. He took my phone. Or it happened too fast. Or I was too scared. Most women aren't thinking about recording or photographing abuse. They're thinking about survival.

The only reason I had the wherewithal to document anything at all was because of my father's background and my own training. I knew evidence might be the only way to stay alive or protect my kids.

Even going to the doctor felt like a risk. If the bruises triggered a report, that could be the end of me.

When the prosecutors reviewed my recordings, they said they could support dozens—maybe hundreds—of charges. But they chose to focus on the "big ones":

- The gun.
- The threats.
- The incidents involving the kids and animals.

We believed it would be enough. That no jury could hear it all and let him walk.

It took almost a year between the time I reported the abuse to the time we were scheduled to go to trial. And then, Mike agreed to a plea deal. We were all relieved, and I asked that they structure something so that he could retain his access to care. The prosecution was chomping at the bit to see what they believed was justice, but considered my request with empathy and agreed.

But when the day came and Mike stood up to plead, he stated, “Your honor, I can’t plead guilty. I didn’t do any of this.” The judge was astounded and had never seen it in his entire career. Mike’s own lawyer looked like he wanted to deck him.

He later told me it was because he wanted me to suffer, to be embarrassed - even if by lies - and what the defense was planning was “evil.”

The trial was postponed for another seven months.

But Mike’s “jury of peers” was composed entirely of male officers and warrant officers. Every juror with a personal connection to domestic violence was dismissed. In the military, rank and loyalty run deep. These were not neutral peers—they were men conditioned to protect their own - especially someone with such an impressive career. Not a single woman sat on the panel.

The defense leaned hard into cultural bias—portraying me as bitter, vengeful, unstable, controlling. That I had made all of this up to sell a book. What struck me most, though, was that the lead defense attorney—a man positioning me as emotionally unstable and opportunistic—was a former

Army Ranger himself. In discussions with JAG staff and my own victim advocate attorney, it seemed that his own client was difficult to manage.

The prosecution couldn't introduce prior behavior unless it was directly tied to the charge. So the jury never heard about the time he pulled a gun on a neighbor. Or waved one in a road rage incident. Or held one to his own head. We couldn't mention the protection orders.

But the defense was allowed to introduce the words of people loyal to Mike and a cascade of accusations without evidence.

DARVO in Uniform

There's a saying often quoted in military circles—especially in Special Operations: **"Admit nothing. Deny everything. Make counteraccusations."**

It likely originated as a tool for POWs and intelligence officers—a way to avoid capture or forced confessions. But in court, that tactic was turned inward. And that's exactly what they did.

It's a strategy also used by both abusers and defense attorneys—so common it has a name: **DARVO**, an acronym coined by psychologist Dr. Jennifer Freyd:

- **Deny:** The abuser denies any wrongdoing or that the

abuse occurred at all.

- **Attack:** The abuser shifts the focus by attacking the victim, questioning their motives or discrediting their testimony via character assisnation

- **Reverse Victim and Offender:** The abuser flips the script, claiming to be the actual victim and portraying the real victim as the abuser. *Freyd, J.J. (1997).*

They even hired a professional body language expert to observe the jury—tracking reactions, advising strategy. It wasn't about the truth. It was about performance. **They put on a show and played the jury like a fiddle.**

The Outcome

I will say that the prosecution was incredible to work with. They were empathetic. They were both combat veterans themselves and like lions in the courtroom. At one point I was afraid the lead prosecutor was going to jump the bench and go after Mike. They did the best they could and I will forever be grateful for their commitment to seeing it though with the resources they had.

But it wasn't enough.

Mike was found not guilty of the gun incident. He was convicted of lesser charges—one a felony for throwing water on me.

And in context, that felony was justified. But out of context? It does sound ridiculous. But that felony conviction was never about water. It was about everything the system ignored.

His punishment? Fourteen days in jail. A two-month reduction in pay. A permanently filed GOMOR and separation under general discharge.

And honestly, I was okay with that. Because I testified. Because I stood up and told the truth. I didn't want him to go to jail or suffer immeasurably. I just wanted my kids and me to be safe—but later learned that charges weren't enough to protect my children.

The prosecution and I had agreed to drop the child and animal abuse charges to spare my son from testifying. We thought the gun case was strong enough.

But it wasn't. And even with a felony on record, the civilian courts still didn't restrict his access to our children. *It was just water.*

Everything I endured. Everything I was able to document. Everything I wasn't. All the years I stayed, believing I could protect them.

It wasn't enough, either.

Left Behind

Even after divorce, the losses continue. There are few

government resources for former military spouses—especially those who don't qualify under the strict 20/20/20 rule.

Health insurance? Gone. Access to the commissary and base services? Gone. Retirement benefits? Only if awarded by a judge—and only in part. Survivor benefits? Only if your former spouse elects to include you.

Even programs like TRICARE or the Survivor Benefit Plan require specific legal action or eligibility windows that many women don't know about—or can't afford to pursue during a contentious divorce.

There is one program called transitional compensation that's available to spouses whose servicemembers were convicted of domestic violence related offenses: three years of a monthly stipend, one free move, and access to tri-care. But that only begins when the service member is actually separated - and can take months afterward to kick in - and only lasts as long as the spouse does not live with the abuser and doesn't re-marry. As of the writing of this book, it's been over 15 months since the trial, and likely another year before Mike is officially separated. The purpose behind transcomp was to help victims move and start over - but bureaucratic tape renders it almost entirely ineffective.

There is no transition assistance for the wife who gave up her career to support his. Who survived abuse but never

spoke out.
No monthly check for the woman who moved ten times in twelve years.
No safety net for the spouse who left because she had to—but still ended up alone, broke, and rebuilding from scratch.

The military cuts the cord cleanly. But most women are left holding the weight of what came before—and what's still ahead.

For all intents and purposes, wives who choose to leave are left behind—and the personal cost to them is exorbitant, *especially if they have children.*

The Cost of Single Parenting

There's no denying that some women in custody disputes are vengeful, petty, or spiteful. But the reality—often overlooked in sensationalized narratives—is that for most women, it is wholly in their own best interest to a) have the marriage work and b) maintain a positive co-parenting relationship if it doesn't. Any other outcome drastically reduces her chances of not only providing adequately for her children but also living a healthy, stable life herself.

Single mothers in the United States face some of the most dire financial and health outcomes of any demographic. More than a quarter of them live below the poverty line—over three times the rate for married-parent households. Wealth disparities are staggering: the Urban Institute reports that single mothers have a median wealth of just

$7,000, compared to over **$50,000** for single fathers and more than **$100,000** for married couples.

Financial instability does not exist in a vacuum—it takes a measurable toll on health. The CDC has found that single mothers are twice as likely to suffer from depression, and they report significantly higher rates of chronic stress, anxiety, and disrupted sleep. Prolonged financial strain has been linked to increased rates of hypertension, autoimmune disease, chronic pain, and higher mortality from all causes—including heart disease, stroke, and cancer. These aren't just "quality of life" issues; they're predictors of lifespan.

The picture is equally sobering for children. Decades of research show that children in homes with both parents present—assuming the absence of abuse—tend to have better outcomes across every major measure: physical and mental health, educational achievement, social adjustment, and lifetime earnings.

So when a woman reaches the point of deciding whether to stay or leave, it's rarely over petty grievances. By the time she makes that choice, the situation is usually dire—severe enough to outweigh the very real costs to her financial security, her health, and her children's futures. The narrative of the "vindictive ex-wife" may make for an easy cultural trope, but the numbers tell a different story: leaving is almost always a last resort, not a strategy.

"If it was really ***that bad****, how could you* ***possibly*** *have stayed so long?"*

Suicide Survivors

The outcome isn't any better if your husband succumbs to invisible wounds here at home. The folded flag, the speeches, the "He was a hero" tributes—they fade quickly.

Retired CSM Will Haddon committed suicide just a month before he was scheduled to speak at a suicide prevention event. The night before he died, he attacked his wife, Sarah, for the first time in their marriage. In the months leading up to his death, she reported paranoid delusions and CTE-like behavior. ***He reached out to the VA repeatedly, only to be met with "we'll call you backs" that never came.***

Though not technically an "operator," Haddon carried his share of blast-wave exposure as a machine-door gunner and continued combat missions up until his retirement. **When Sarah called to report his death, the VA hung up on her.**

She had already given up her own military career to support his. Yet when he passed, she lost everything. His retirement. Their benefits. **The government even deducted the retirement and disability funds from their bank account for the month that he died - and then only paid Sarah for the days that he was alive.** What's left for her and their children is a small monthly DIC payment—an amount that doesn't even match what transcomp is supposed to offer domestic violence survivors.

All of it—erased—because our government refuses to acknowledge the impact combat operations and training have on the brain. If a soldier bled out from visible wounds stateside, his family would receive full benefits. But if the wounds are invisible, like PTSD or BWE, the system looks away. It buries the family alongside the service member.

No matter what we do—how much we love, how well we hold the home-front down, how loyal we are, how quiet we stay, how much we endure, how much evidence we have, or how much of our live and our families we lose—this is a war we were never meant to win.

Deliverance doesn't mean immediate peace. Israel learned that in the desert. Freedom didn't feel like freedom at first—it felt like hunger, thirst, uncertainty, and even war. They grumbled about manna. They longed for Egypt. Even slavery felt easier than the wilderness.

I know that feeling.

I struggled with severe anxiety. I slept with Kevlar behind my head because from the woods behind our house, he had a perfect line of sight to where I lay. The windows framed exactly where my head would be. I dragged the mattress onto the floor.

I checked parking lots. Counted how many turns the cars behind me made. Changed routes more times than I can remember. I went into debt to feed

my kids. Tried to keep my business afloat under the crushing weight of both civil and military legal proceedings. I raised three small children with no family nearby, while fighting through relentless autoimmune flares.

And still, I wrestled with the decision to divorce Mike. Even after the gun incident. Even after it escalated to the dog and the kids. I still clung to hope—that something, anything, might shake him. That maybe therapy would change him. That maybe we'd find miraculous healing. That somehow, we could be safe.

He went to multiple therapies. He learned all the right words. We even attempted reconciliation—twice. And that became ammunition against me in court-martial: If it was really that bad, why would you ever go back?

When I realized his words weren't for healing but for control—just a tactic to keep me from testifying—I was heartbroken. And more afraid than ever.

But God showed up. He gave me courage that could not have come from anywhere else, because it certainly wasn't in me. I didn't want this cup. But I had no choice.

Looking back now, I see how much I was like Israel

in the desert. God was leading me out—not just from physical danger, but from spiritual enslavement. From idolatry. From a marriage that could kill me and gave Him no glory. From a system that used people for profit. That chose greed over God-given dignity.

But there were days, even weeks, when I grumbled about manna. I longed for Egypt. For easier days. And if Mike was really getting help, maybe it would be better for my boys to grow up with two parents—even in Egypt—than to wander in the desert with me.

The truth was: He had delivered me from not just an Egypt, but Sodom - a place of total destruction and death - and I still looked back.

But thank God for His mercy.

Because when the bigger picture came into view—when I finally saw what He had saved me from—I began to glimpse the freedom He intended all along.

Freedom in the truth.

In telling it, and in trusting His promises—no matter the outcome, no matter what was left at my feet or lay ahead.

My voice was small at first. Broken, halting, barely there. But it was still there. And no threat Mike made—or the men he promised would kill me if he couldn't—could silence me until God said my time was done.

I had children to raise. And an awful truth to tell:

It really was that bad.

It really is that bad.

Not just for me—but for countless soldiers suffering in silence.

Not just for my family—but for many others like us.

Even for Mike himself.

And like Israel in the wilderness, I had to keep walking. To keep speaking. To keep repenting for when I started to turn to idols or looking back toward what God had delivered me from. Because silence may feel safe, but it's still slavery. The wilderness is frightening—yet it is also where God provides, where He teaches us to trust Him one day at a time.

Chapter Nine – Caught in the Crossfire

Reilly was barely two when he put the first hole in the wall. I didn't understand the anger in my toddler—anger that seemed far too big for his small body. At the time, things at home weren't even "that bad." Not yet.

When I became the primary target of abuse, Reilly sometimes became the witness. I did everything I could to keep him away from it. I thought I was catching it all. I thought he couldn't hear. I was wrong.

As he grew, I noticed a shift—he was becoming a target, too. I stepped in. Took the heat. Thought it was enough. It wasn't.

It often took him days to find the courage to tell me if something happened—first quietly, then through sobs. In those first months in Tennessee, there were incidents, but no marks. No proof. He begged me not to leave him alone with his dad—not even for a grocery run. We created a code word for when he needed to talk in private.

And if I called CPS, we could all wind up dead.

Then it happened - I was home, and I heard it: They were arguing about bedtime in his room. Suddenly, a hollow whop.

Reilly came screaming down the stairs, holding his stomach.

No marks—but this time, I heard it.
I called the cops.

The line had been crossed.

I thought leaving his father would help, but Reilly only spiraled.
He missed "good dad."

Mike told him it was all my fault, that I was keeping them apart. He called me a "whore bitch" during one call. That was the first time Reilly punched me.

The rages came fast after that—trashing the house, fighting neighborhood kids, attacking me, acting out at school.
Therapy.
ADHD diagnosis.

Meds.
Hospitalization for suicidal thoughts.

Nothing worked.

After discharge, he declined again. I called every therapy office between Clarksville and Nashville. Six-month waitlists—minimum. Because he hadn't attempted suicide again, he wasn't considered "critical."
There weren't enough providers on post.
There was nothing.

His doctors suggested I adjudicate him. He was eight.

As a last-ditch effort, I thought about getting a horse. I knew the healing power of horses from my own childhood. I'd read about a program out west using mustangs to rehabilitate prisoners—recidivism was almost nonexistent. It wasn't backed by much science yet, but I was out of options.

I found a mustang for $300. Field board was $120. Maybe I could swing it.

She was halterbroke, thin, kept in a 12x12 stall. When I saw her with a little boy, she melted. She was perfect.

But the numbers terrified me. That night, I went to my room, got on my knees, and prayed: "Lord, I need a really clear sign. If this is the right thing to do, please help me know."

I walked into Reilly's room.

He was hanging out the second-story window by his fingertips—trying to kill himself.

We brought the horse home as soon as we could. She tolerated me—but melted for Reilly. Groomed him. Softened for him. Within two weeks, he made a complete 180. She was an answer to one prayer—but we had many more ahead.

The guardian ad litem (GAL), a lawyer meant to represent my children's best interests—had over 20 contacts with

Mike and his parents and four or fewer with me. I emailed asking what she needed. No response.

She recommended reintegration. My lawyer said, "He schmoozed her. We could do worse in court."

I had voice recordings of my children sobbing after visits. Reilly's disclosures about abuse I never knew was happening years before. Those were almost inadmissible in court. Charges were dropped at courts-martial to protect Reilly from testifying. The most serious charges came back "not guilty." Nothing stopped Mike from getting 50/50 custody.

Right before the divorce finalized, another incident at Mike's—"just verbal," but terrifying. The GAL ignored it and continued to recommend reintegration.

Maybe they were right—maybe things would get better without me in the picture. Mike had done family therapy, completed FAP programs, and finished substance abuse treatment. I had held him accountable. That had to be enough... right?

Three months later, the boys came home with marks on Reilly's neck and flushed cheeks. They said they'd had fun. I studied him. He insisted there was nothing wrong. As a mom of three, I can't account for most of their bumps and bruises, so I told myself the red cheeks might just be from a flu or strep coming on.

A month later, Reilly broke down. Said his dad slapped him

but begged me not to tell. When he left for school, I filed with CID. They indexed it.

Kentucky denied my request for a protection order—no jurisdiction. With paperwork in hand, I took the boys to the Tennessee courthouse. We had dropped off paperwork before and I told them it was just a formality, but Reilly knew something was off. Back home, I told him the truth: I had to speak up before things got worse.

He looked down at the floor and started to cry, "It already did."
That's when he told me—his father had choked him twice and slapped his face each time. The first time, over breakfast casserole. The second, after Reilly said "f*** you" in terror and defiance.

CID opened an investigation.

Kentucky CPS closed theirs as "unfounded." No photos. CPS had to take them directly.

The Army's Incident Determination Committee ruled it physical child abuse—command refused a protective order.

In court, Mike admitted slapping Reilly, claiming it was discipline. In Tennessee, a teacher doing that is guilty of assault. A parent? "Corporal punishment."

Reilly testified—calm, clear: yes, it happened. Yes, he still loved his dad. Yes, he wanted him to get help. He was brave.

The judge conceded "something happened" and dismissed the order.

We tried to modify custody. Court was set for when I was already scheduled to be away for my mother's wedding and meetings at te Senate on this very subject matter. My lawyer assured me we'd have it rescheduled - it wasn't. Case dismissed. I was ordered to pay Mike's legal fees.

I did everything right.

I listened to my son.

I fought for him.

He did everything right.

He told the truth.

And we were both punished.

FAP still hasn't released IDC records. Multiple senators have ignored my emails and 15-page incident report with evidence files. The military declined to prosecute.

If I let him go to his dad's house, he could be killed. If I kept him back, I could lose custody—and he could be killed anyway.

The gun incident alone makes Mike 20 times more likely to commit homicide. Choking increases the risk sevenfold. The risk that he kills his own child? Through the roof.

We're all being punished.

Because of the myth. Because the abuse "wasn't bad enough."
Because I stayed too long. Because I considered reuniting. Because my son is articulate for his age—he was disbelieved, and I was accused of coaching. Even though his therapists repeatedly note his extraordinary acuity with language and above-his-age understanding of people and situations.

I did what any good mother should do under the law—and Reilly was thrown right back into the path of our collective abuser.

This isn't just our story. What happened to Reilly is horrifying—but it isn't unusual. His story reflects a larger, well-documented failure by both the military and our civilian courts to protect, let alone adequately intervene for, the children who bear the highest costs of war.

And I need to be clear: combat service—even with a PTSD diagnosis—does not automatically make someone a dangerous parent. I know many combat veterans who are devoted, loving fathers—men who fight every day to manage their symptoms and shield their families from the worst of their struggles. PTSD is not a moral failing, and it is not a guarantee of abuse. The danger comes when trauma, brain injury, or substance misuse go untreated for years—and when the systems meant to protect families fail to act before that struggle spills over onto spouses and children, who are often disbelieved and then thrown back into the line of fire when they finally find the courage to speak.

What We Didn't Know

It's a common thread in military families: children as young as eighteen months acting out, struggling in school, or sinking into depression. (Gewirtz et al., 2010; Lester et al., 2010).Over the years, I've met more parents than not whose sons and daughters have been hospitalized for suicidal ideation, who carry symptoms that look like complex PTSD, who sit in therapy week after week—hurting in ways their parents don't know how to heal, and in ways local resources can't always reach.

Every April, the military reminds us to "wear purple" for the Month of the Military Child, to honor the sacrifices our kids make for our country. But our children never signed up for this. They were born into it. They never consented to being herded through a system that forgets them—and they will pay for the rest of their lives for what that system failed to see, failed to stop, and failed to repair.

One out of every four high school–aged military children in California reported seriously considering suicide. *(Cozza et al., 2019)*. Research shows that the greater the cumulative time a parent is deployed, the more likely a child is to struggle with mental-health concerns. Special Operations forces operate under some of the most sustained and demanding deployment and training cycles in the military, yet there are no programs specifically designed for Special

Operations children. The programs that do exist are underfunded, understaffed, and overwhelmed—and they fall far short of providing the resources and expertise our children urgently need. (Chandra et al., 2013; Cozza & Lerner, 2013).

As Army.mil reported: *"There have even been reports of higher levels of suicidal ideations among children who have been through numerous parental deployments,"* said Dr. Stephen Cozza, a retired colonel, psychiatrist, and associate director of the Center for the Study of Traumatic Stress at the Uniformed Services University in Bethesda, Maryland. He went on to add: *"The majority of children are doing well despite those challenges."*

I'm sorry, but if one in four kids is reporting suicidal ideation, that is not "doing well." The bar for their collective well-being is in hell.

And it starts early. Even before a child can put feelings into words, research has documented that babies show developmental and behavioral issues tied directly to parental deployment. Regression in toilet training, disrupted sleep, and aggression are all common—and these behaviors often intensify with each subsequent deployment cycle.

The statistics don't get better.

Military children have higher ACE (Adverse Childhood Experiences) scores on average than their civilian peers.

Children with four or more ACEs are twelve times more likely to attempt suicide, ten times more likely to use injection drugs, and four times more likely to experience depression. *(Felitti et al., 1998)*. My son Reilly has an ACE score of eight—which puts his risk of suicide thirty to fifty-one times higher than someone with zero ACEs. But there was nowhere for him to go.

In military families—especially in high-tempo communities like Special Operations—ACE scores can climb rapidly. A single household can stack multiple ACE categories in a matter of years: repeated deployments and parental absences, exposure to combat trauma, emotional neglect during reintegration, witnessing domestic violence, and, in some cases, direct physical or emotional abuse. Add in the stress of frequent moves, inconsistent schooling, and gaps in medical or mental-health care, and many military children reach the "high-risk" ACE threshold before they've even entered middle school.

And if parent dies by suicide before a child turns 18, that child's risk of also dying by suicide later in life is about three times higher *(Wilcox et al. 2010; Kuramoto et al. 2009)*. If we are losing an estimated 22-44 veterans per day to suicide, we must face the ripple effect on their children, too. This crisis is not confined to service members—it perpetuates generational trauma and loss when left unaddressed (*Department of Veterans Affairs 2023; National Academies of Sciences, Engineering, and Medicine 2019; Ramchand et al. 2011).*

Certain risk factors carry particular weight. According to the original CDC–Kaiser Permanente Adverse Childhood Experiences Study, having a parent with post-traumatic stress disorder (PTSD) qualifies as living with a household member with mental illness—counting as one ACE. Having a parent who struggles with substance misuse—alcohol or drugs—qualifies as living with a substance-abusing household member—counting as another ACE. When both are present, that's two separate ACE points before considering any other adversity. In Special Operations homes, where PTSD and substance misuse frequently co-occur, this stacking effect happens quickly and often.

And for children like Reilly, the compounding effect isn't theoretical—it's a measurable, predictable path toward lifelong harm. The CDC reports that individuals with four or more ACEs face significantly increased risk of chronic disease, mental health disorders, and premature death. Specifically, higher ACE scores are linked to increased lifetime risk of heart disease, stroke, autoimmune disease, diabetes, obesity, and even cancer—alongside a dramatically higher risk of suicide, depression, and substance misuse in adulthood. And the Department of Defense and Department of Veterans Affairs already have decades of research showing that unaddressed parental PTSD, substance misuse, and domestic violence directly and predictably harm children—often for life. Yet there are no targeted, adequately resourced programs to identify high-ACE-score military children early, intervene effectively, or protect them in custody disputes.

Just witnessing domestic violence counts as one ACE. Research shows that babies perceive their mothers as an extension of themselves—and when a mother is assaulted, the infant's brain internalizes that assault as if it happened to them. *(Winnicott, 1960; Schore, 2001; Levendosky et al., 2015; Martinez-Torteya et al., 2017; Scheeringa, 2012).* This changes the brain's structure and function—not only in infants, but in older children as well. Witnessing violence leads to measurable dysregulation, disrupts growth in multiple brain regions, and can even cause epigenetic changes—alterations in gene expression that can be passed to the next generation.

If domestic violence is occurring in the home and a spouse elects to leave, the military and civilian courts often fail to protect the children *(Leadership Council on Child Abuse & Interpersonal Violence).* In the United States, 58,000 children every year are court-ordered into unsupervised contact with an abusive parent following custody litigation. In the overwhelming majority (70–90%) of cases where custody is disputed based on allegations of abuse, the alleged abuser is granted custody and/or unsupervised visitation *(Meier, 2016).*

Yet protective parents who report abuse are statistically more likely to lose custody than those who remain silent *(Meier, 2019).*

In my own case, my sons' father hurled baseless allegations in court—that I encouraged homosexuality in my children because I allowed my five-year-old to paint his nails when he asked (developmentally appropriate), that I was "coaching" them, that I was "turning them against him." There was no evidence. In fact, I have evidence to the contrary. But it didn't matter. Judicial reliance on "parental alienation" claims has repeatedly resulted in courts siding with abusive parents.*(Meier, 2020; UN Special Rapporteur on Violence Against Women, 2023; NCJFCJ Bench Guide)*

In Tennessee, it is considered assault if a coach, teacher, or any other adult slaps a child in the face—unless that adult is the child's parent. Parents are legally allowed to strike their children in the face as "corporal punishment." That is not logic. That is institutionally sanctioned domestic violence.

And my therapist, who had worked in the court system, was right: it didn't matter what he did to me as long as I was still alive—he would still get at least partial custody. And he did.

Despite decades of research documenting how often intimate partner violence escalates toward children. *(Appel & Holden, 1998; Thackeray et al., 2023; Pearson et al., 2023).*

Despite knowing how even witnessing abuse can damage children—often for life.

An abuser's right to parent should never outweigh a child's right to be safe.

But as of today, it does.

And that is inexcusable.

It is an evil we can no longer tolerate if we want to claim even the smallest shred of moral competence.

And that is why this fight is personal. It isn't just policy failure—it's the lived reality of my child - and children, and thousands like them. This isn't theory. This is our home. Our life. Our battle.

Egypt murdered the sons of the Israelites to weaken them. Pharaoh wasn't just cruel — he was calculated. If he could cut off the children, he could cripple the future.

Our own systems have done the same, though with suits and gavels instead of swords. By refusing to act, by sanitizing abuse as "discipline," by dismissing trauma as "not bad enough," they are condemning children to lives cut short by suicide, addiction, and despair. They may not swing the blade themselves, but their neglect does the killing all the same.

And God sees it. Scripture is clear: He hears the cries of the oppressed, especially children. He judged Egypt for what they did to His people's sons, and He will not ignore what is happening to ours.

Like Moses's mother, I have tried to shield my son

in every way I can — and sometimes, it feels like I'm setting him adrift in a basket, praying he survives a river I cannot control. But the God who heard Israel's children crying out is the same God who hears mine and so many other parents facing the same, horrifying risks. The same God who raised up Moses to confront Pharaoh still raises up voices to confront the systems that sanctify harm today.

And that's why I cannot stay silent. Because silence only empowers Pharaoh to perpetuate pain. And my God is not silent — He is a warrior, not of wrath but of rescue. The one who split seas, toppled empires, and set captives free stands with the children the system has thrown to the wolves.

Our may be caught in the crossfire, but they are not abandoned. And our God calls us to fight for them - by breaking the chains of silence.

"Praise be to the Lord my Rock,
who trains my hands for war,
my fingers for battle."
— Psalm 144:1

Chapter Ten: Reckoning & Redemption

If a private corporation knowingly exposed its employees to harmful hazards, punished them for seeking medical care, blocked access to treatment, hid the scope of harm, and retaliated against family members who spoke out—it would trigger lawsuits, congressional hearings, and public outrage.

Yet the U.S. military has done exactly this to its service members and their families—and we've heard virtually nothing.

Crickets from Congress.

Crickets from the Senate.

Crickets from the media.

The consensus is that nothing can be done. Most operators and their families that I've spoken with feel resigned to face a system that is designed to keep them quiet - and suffering. "The machine is too big." It's immovable. And when policies are implemented, they are wrapped in so much red tape that they're rendered ineffective at best, but often detrimental. There wasn't a single active-duty service member I've spoken with who believes that there are policies that protect them. But there are—or at least, there should be.

The Reckoning: Policies They Wrote — and Broke

DoDI 6055.01 — DoD Safety & Occupational Health: Policy requires hazard communication, but in practice, behavioral risks like PTSD, TBI, and BWE are often omitted from briefings to service members and their families—creating a dangerous blind spot."

DoDI 6490.13 — Comprehensive Brain Health Assessments: Mandates baseline/post-exposure neurocognitive scans for high-risk MOSs. Broken: Many never receive them; missing data blocks early treatment and VA claims.

DoDI 6400.06 — Domestic Abuse Response: Requires education on the Family Advocacy Program (FAP) and confidential help. Broken: Many spouses never told FAP exists or how to reach it safely.

DoDI 1300.06 — Mental Health Fitness Determinations: Requires evaluation when conditions may impair performance or endanger others. Broken: Operators with severe PTSD/TBI remain in roles without adequate treatment.

DoDI 1322.34 — DV Prevention Training: Requires commanders and leaders to know DV risk factors and victim safety protocols. Broken: Leaders and SFRG reps receive no meaningful DV-specific training for combat-related behavioral risks.

DoDI 5154.31 – Armed Forces Medical Examiner: Requires accurate service-connected death determinations. Broken: Suicides tied to service injuries often classified in a manner that denies survivor benefits.

38 C.F.R. § 3.303 & 3.304 – Service-Connection for Disabilities: Requires recognition of service-linked conditions with evidence. Broken: Lack of DoD documentation for TBI/BWE/PTSD shifts proof burden to veterans.

M21-1 Adjudication Manual – PTSD & MST Claims: Requires full development of claims, even without formal reports. Broken: Survivors face denials without full investigation.

VA/DoD Clinical Practice Guidelines – PTSD, mTBI, SUD: Requires evidence-based, coordinated care. Broken: Treatments are inconsistently offered, tracked, or available.

These aren't bureaucratic oversights. Every broken policy has a human cost—a life cut short, a family destroyed. The gap between what is written and what is enforced is where the damage happens.

This is the hidden war—and it is claiming more lives than any battlefield.

Redemption: What Needs to Change – Now – To Save Lives

We don't need more studies. We don't need another decade of commissions and task forces. The answers are already on the table—what's missing is the courage to act.

These are the changes that could save lives immediately:

Baseline & Ongoing Brain Scans – Enforce neurocognitive testing for all high-risk MOSs from entry to separation.

Early Retirement for High-Risk MOSs – Shorten timelines in high-trauma jobs with full benefits.

Access to Alternative Therapies — Remove command vetoes and fund proven treatments like TMS, equine therapy, and psychedelic-assisted therapy.

Mandatory Post-Deployment Programs – Make post-deployment mental health care automatic and confidential.

Peer Advocacy System — Pair troops with trained peers to navigate the care process.

Annual SOF Review Panel — Protected, confidential briefings from randomly selected operators and spouses to Congress.

Command Evaluations — Anonymous subordinate-led reviews tied to promotion decisions.

Extend OSHA Protections — Apply core workplace hazard disclosure laws to active duty military, ensuring that they are educated on the physical, mental, and behavioral health impact of BWE, c-PTSD, and TBI/mTBI

On-Post Safe Housing — Immediate, secure DV survivor housing on every installation.

Mandatory Rights & Resource Briefings — Pre-DEERS enrollment or card reissuance education for spouses and dependents on risks, rights, and confidential help.

Expand Mental Health Access & Child Care — More providers, telehealth, and on-demand child care for appointments.

Reform Transitional Compensation — Start payments at charges, end remarriage penalty, and expand eligibility.

DV Legal Costs Tax Credit — Refundable credit for documented DV-related legal expenses.

Gold Star Status for Service-Connected Suicide — Recognize suicide tied to service injuries as a line-of-duty death.

Thoughts on Policy and Implementation

Too often, policies that shape service members' lives are

drafted in conference rooms far removed from the realities of the battlefield, the barracks, or the family home. The people writing the rules rarely live under them—and the result is predictable: policies that look good on paper but fail in practice.

Real change requires operator and family voices at the table from the start. Their input must shape the design, not just be sought as an afterthought. That means involving them **before approval** to identify choke points, and keeping them engaged **during implementation** to ensure the system works as intended.

It also means creating safeguards so that care is truly accessible: no waitlists that stretch for months, no opaque referral processes, no confusing chains of command that intimidate people into silence. Just as critically, it means ensuring that **no one faces career damage, social ostracism, or other forms of retaliation** for seeking the services they have earned—and that our country owes them in spades.

When those directly affected are not only consulted but empowered to help shape, monitor, and refine policy, two things happen:

1. **Fewer people slip through the cracks.**
2. **The system begins to rebuild trust** with the community it exists to serve.

Anything less is lip service—and lip service doesn't save lives - it has historically ended them.

The time for studies and speeches has passed. The only question now is whether our leaders will stand with those who served—or stand in the way - and whether we have the courage to hold our institutions and their leaders to account.

Jesus was crucified. His disciples were murdered. None recanted. Truth almost always comes with a price—and it is often astronomical.

The Israelites fled into the desert. They left behind everything they knew, and after years of wandering, they came upon even greater battles. They fought the Amalekites, the Amorites, the Midianites, the Moabites, the Canaanites—tribes stronger and better established than they were. Freedom was not handed to them. They had to fight for it, step by step, battle by battle.

If we love our soldiers and families—if we care about national readiness and moral integrity—silence is not an option. Not anymore. We must fight for them.

We must be brave despite our fear.

We must understand that this, too, is war.

For decades, the DoD and VA have waged psychological warfare against our own—against those who fight for us and the families who stand beside them. It is time to fight back.

Fight for those silenced too long.

Fight to name what has already been lost. Fight for the future of our children and our country.

This is not just policy—it is covenant. We are fighting for holy ground. For the land promised when we swore to defend one another, when we bound ourselves as a nation to care for those who bear the wounds of our wars.

Like Nehemiah rebuilding Jerusalem's wall under constant threat, we must build with one hand and defend with the other. Because this fight is sacred. The lives of soldiers and families are holy ground—and that ground has been trampled by neglect and betrayal long enough.

God is not mocked, and His justice does not fail. What He requires of us is clear:

"Learn to do good; seek justice, correct oppression; bring justice to the fatherless, plead the widow's cause." — Isaiah 1:17

"Have I not commanded you? Be strong and courageous. Do not be frightened, and do not be dismayed, for the Lord your God is with you wherever you go." — Joshua 1:9

Chapter Eleven: Last Words

It would be easy to write Mike off as an anomaly – a "bad apple" who slipped through the cracks. Truth be told, I don't know if he was ever a sheepdog, if he was always a wolf, or if he was a sheepdog who became a wolf. I do know I'm not alone in what I observed and experienced. An overwhelming number of wives I spoke to over the years were dealing with husbands who had changed – many of them in ways that were dangerous to themselves at a minimum, but that often accompanied danger to their own family members as well.

In the end, it all came down to accountability. I couldn't force Mike get help or change, and when someone is that far gone, the consequences have to outweigh the rewards of continuing their behavior. That was the guiding insight a retired operator shared with me, and it heavily factored into my decision to testify at his court-martial. It's also why we must continue to hold those who commit violent crimes against their family members accountable.

Not because we hate them. Not because it erases what they sacrificed, endured, and accomplished for our country – because I don't believe it does, not by a long shot. But because there comes a point when accountability is the only way to protect them – and others – from themselves.

We can hold people accountable and still love them. I hate what Mike did. There were times I was furious, others when I was grief-stricken to the point of true speechlessness, nights when I lay on the floor before God and prayed, through sobs, for mercy and for the awful cup to pass from us all, and others when I felt nothing at all. But I don't hate Mike. We can hate the sin without hating the sinner. And if we truly love them — if we want what is best for them and for everyone their life touches — then we must hold them accountable. That is not betrayal, vengeance, self-righteousness, or anger. That is love with boundaries strong enough to save lives.

Ultimately, it doesn't matter what or who Mike is.

What matters is that he *knew* something was wrong—and didn't feel like he could get help.

What matters is that there were no truly safe resources for me, and no education to explain why it was happening in our home.

What matters is how it impacted my children—and that they are *still* in serious danger.

What matters is that Mike wasn't - and isn't - the only one who feels stuck between two losing options.

We are not the minority.

There are *so many more* service members and families still quietly suffering.

I wrestled for nearly a year with how to finish this book. I wanted a tidy ending—some kind of resolution to hand the reader. But the truth is, there isn't one. This story isn't over.

Right now, a child is cowering under furniture. A service member is thinking about going home from work and pulling a trigger. A wife is wondering what will happen when the day is over and he pours a drink. Right now, the systems meant to protect them are still failing. And the longer we look away, the more we guarantee the same pain for the next generation.

There were many women I spoke with who were inexplicably angry—and they have every reason to be. There is a necessity for righteous anger.

Several told me there should be harsher penalties for these crimes and focused heavily on judicial outcomes. While I don't necessarily disagree, addressing abuse only after the fact is triage—and triage will never end until we identify and address the root causes of why so many of our families are suffering.

When you're firing a pistol, many factors determine where the round lands—if it lands at all. Grip, anticipation, posture, even breathing all play a role. A trained eye can diagnose the shooter's issues by studying the shot group—the pattern left on the target. You don't move the target to fix the problem; you address the shooter's fundamentals.

Suicide rates, domestic violence, long-term service member and dependent health outcomes, children in crisis, staffing shortages, and retention problems are the shot group. But the DoD, VA, and our government aren't even looking at the target—because doing so would force them to take responsibility for what's happening at the trigger pull.

In all likelihood, their failure comes down to cost. Follow the money, and you'll find the answer. What is "saved" by failing to adequately treat and support service members and their families is stained with blood—the literal cost of a system that chooses budgets over lives.

We cannot truly address domestic violence or the suicide rate until we address soldiers' foundations, exposures, and injuries at their source. That's the trigger pull.

Healing can only begin when we hold the DoD and VA accountable for their criminal lack of disclosure to service members and their families.

Because at the end of the day, accountability isn't just for the individual who commits the violence—it's for the institutions that enable it through silence and malicious neglect. We can love our service members, honor their sacrifice, and still demand that the systems responsible for their well-being tell them the truth, give them real support, and intervene before their pain destroys them or the people they love.

Love without boundaries is not love at all. And if we truly care about our soldiers, their families, and the future of our country, we must be willing to hold both people and systems accountable—not to punish, but to protect.

I used to think all of this was random. Chaotic. A string of failures and wrong turns that had left me broken and off-course.

I flunked out of college after a head injury—something I carried like a quiet shame. My family couldn't see the crippling migraines and bursts of blue light in my vision that left me bed-ridden after reading just a few lines of text. Instead of understanding, they came down hard. So I ran. I married a soldier in the 82nd, gave my brain time to heal and went on to complete basic law enforcement training. But just two weeks after graduation, my hands went predominantly numb. The feeling eventually returned, but in a matter of days I had lost a potential career in law enforcement and, shortly after, my marriage. It felt like everything I tried to do that was good ended the same way—shattered and thrown back at me like a grenade.

But those losses led me to the Q Course, where I took a civilian role. We were sitting around a campfire one fall evening out at KK2, waiting for a raid to kick off. A member of the cadre named Paul—someone I'd just been assigned to but had never worked with before—turned to me and asked

how I felt about the Bible.

There was one in my pack, underlined and scarred with frustration and indignation. I'd stolen it from a hotel room in college as a quiet act of rebellion after repeated encounters with Christians whose faith seemed rooted in hatred, judgment, and self-service. I believed in a good and loving God—but not the way this text or its people portrayed Him. I'd begun highlighting every passage that felt wrong, hypocritical, or cruel.

Just a couple of hours earlier, I had been venting to a coworker during route recon about how stupid it all seemed. He wasn't a Christian either. Paul had no idea.

Word around camp was that Paul was a pastor, and I was curious how he could possibly defend such a text.

That night, I became a Christian.

He and his wife, Becky, would later become my second son's godparents.

Ten years after that night at Mackall, in the early stages of writing this book, I called Paul to ask for help clarifying a phrase used in operator circles. We talked about the subject matter and what the guys were facing. Then he paused and said, "Well!

Thank you for choosing Blacksmith Publishing!"

I knew he wrote books. I didn't know he owned the company that published them.

That's when I realized — I hadn't failed. Or maybe I did. But it didn't matter, because God had a plan.

I never wanted to go to college in the first place - at least, not right away; my sights were set on the military or the Peace Corps. My family threatened to disown me if I didn't go, and I eventually conceded.

Twenty years later, my favorite professor and mentor introduced me to his wife, a researcher named Meg Olmert, whose work on how trauma rewires the brain would shape everything I'd come to witness and understand. He cheered me on through the hardest seasons of writing and was a source of encouragement when I was buried under the data, the weight, and the never-ending heartbreak of it all.

The subject control and arrest techniques I thought I'd never use helped me de-escalate, survive, and escape the day a gun was pressed into my skull.

The pain of that marriage gave me the children I would do anything to protect.

And it was the men of the 82nd—their suffering, their decline, their silence—that ignited the research that would eventually become this book.

Service members I'd met over the years acted like whales—resurfacing at just the right moment, checking in, swallowing me whole, and spitting me out exactly when I had thrown this book away and was actively running from it. And every time, they'd say the same thing: "Kate, you have to write this."

None of it was wasted.
None of it was random.

Maybe God opened the door for Mike to change.
Maybe He knew he wouldn't.
But He put people in place.
He put me in place.
And He brought me through it — not just to survive, but to speak.

The research behind this book — if it were all printed, would measure nearly three feet tall, stacked vertically. But if I've learned anything, it's this:

God is good.
God is love.
And love is not silent.
It compels us to sacrifice.

It compels us to act.
It compels us to wrestle with the darkness — in ourselves and in the world around us.

This is not an anti-war book. In Scripture, God commanded His people to confront and dismantle cultures that destroyed their children for the sake of gain — a just war.

Today, we face a quieter but no less deadly version in our own nation — not with altars, but with policies that knowingly sacrifices our sons and daughters on our own homefront.

So I ask you to have courage, to act, to wage war with me — not with violence, but with love.

Not with arrows and swords, but with your voice and your words.

I pray, and hope, in Jesus' name, that it is finally

Enough.

For we do not wrestle against flesh and blood, but against the rulers, against the authorities, against the cosmic powers over this present darkness, against the spiritual forces of evil in the heavenly places. -Ephesians 6:12

Acknowledgements

To those who tried to bury me: your conscience is yours to carry. I pray you find peace and wish you well — truly. What you carry is between you and God, not me.

And to those who chose instead to lift me up, to stand beside me, and to carry part of the weight—these acknowledgements are for you.

To the 2022 1B Nightshift: Clarksville PD and SRT — for your incredible professionalism, kindness, and empathy on one of the worst nights of our lives. Your humanity in the middle of crisis remains a beacon of light I return to when the world feels dark.

To the WCEM teachers, counselors, nurse, and staff — you have been part of our village from day one, and I cannot thank you enough for your grace, kindness, and guidance through some of the heaviest days. Thank you for loving my kids as your own, and for holding me so many times through the storm.

To the researchers and professionals who generously shared articles and insights I couldn't access on my own, and who have dedicated their life's work to understanding and documenting the damage — this would not be possible without you. Thank you for making sense of the chaos. Your work matters more than you may ever know.

To the Operators, Combat Veterans, and family members who bravely shared your stories and experiences, offered your support, connected me with others, helped course-correct my ideas, and encouraged me to keep going — you helped me find my voice again so I could speak for those who can't. This book exists because of your courage, your insight, and your unwavering love for your country and those who serve.

To the CID agents who believed me, the Special Victims' Counselors, Victim Advocates, prosecution team, and SJA staff who stood in the gap and did the hard work of seeking justice — your courage, dedication, selflessness, and grit inspire me every day. Thank you for reminding me that there are courageous people behind the scenes, often unseen, who truly care and are willing to do the work to see justice served.

To Lexy, Charly, and the Agents of MM — thank you for showing up, making me laugh when I needed it most, and believing in me while I was still figuring out how to put one foot in front of the other. Thank you for not giving up on me when the weight felt unbearable, for reminding me I'm not alone in this fight, and for standing your ground — with and for me — when so many workplaces would have slammed the door.

To my incredible clients — thank you for trusting me, even in the middle of chaos, to take care of you and protect your interests. Your faith in me during some of the most difficult seasons has meant more than you know and a great encouragement. We wouldn't be standing without you.

To my family, friends, and neighbors — for the meals, the childcare, the phone calls, the "just checking in" texts, for loving me and being there no matter where my head and heart were, and for giving me grace when I disappeared for weeks to write — I am grateful beyond words and could not have gotten through the last few years without your love and support.

To my parents:

Mom — this took a heavy toll on you, too. Thank you for loving me, for still showing up, and for being a safe space for us when we needed it most. Thank you for teaching us how to love people even when they've hurt us, to hold on to kindness through pain, and to notice where others are hurting even when they don't have the words.

Dad — my first editor, I could never have put two words together without your help and instruction. Thank you for showing me the importance of fighting for what is good, right, and just, no matter the threat or who stood against you. Thank you for dedicating your life to protecting others and for always moving with strength, faith, and kindness. You are always missed, but forever close in my heart.

To Stacy Bannerman: Thank you for picking up the phone. For being the first to light the torch, sound the alarm, show up for the families, and for all the ways you've helped pull us through and out of the darkness. Everything is fine!

To S.J. – thank you for sitting with me through some of the hardest parts of this book's creation, for your patience with the late nights and heavy days, for reminding me to breathe, for telling me over and over again that I was always enough to begin with, and for giving me the freedom to fight.

To J.J. and "the Kids" – thank you for getting me out of the house and reminding me that the world moves on and that there's hope for the future. I couldn't have finished this without the laughter and the late-night talks around kitchen tables and bonfires. Thank you for being our family where we had none and for giving my heart and mind a safe place – with safe people – to reflect, rest, and reset.

To my Publisher – thank you for believing in this story and its purpose, for trusting me to tell it my way, for your patience through the two-year delay in finishing it, and for being the one who first led me to faith in Christ.

To My Boys – I love you more than life. I hope, if you read this one day, you know how much of this was for your future, and for future generations, too. Thank you for endless laughs and reminding me that there is always beauty and joy - even in the darkness. I would have given up a long time ago if it weren't for your love and silliness.

And to my God and King – who held me together when I thought I'd shatter. Who carried me when I could not take one more step. Who gave me a purpose in the middle of the wreckage. Who provided when I doubted, gave me grace when I was scared to trust, who is a pillar of smoke in the day, a pillar of fire at night, and who walks with me every day. All glory to You.

Sources

Christ said He did not come to bring peace, but a sword – one that separates truth from lies and the love of God from hypocrisy. In that same spirit, this book comes not in peace, but with receipts: evidence of what too many Operators and their families have carried in silence. A silence that has cost far too many lives while those in power counted votes, dollars, and careers.

Failure to acknowledge and disclose this research – while leaving service members and their families to feel 'less than' for suffering the consequences of war, or to wonder what is wrong with them when the information was there all along but withheld – is not only institutional gaslighting, it is a morally reprehensible betrayal of the very principles on which our country was founded: integrity, honor, and justice.

Without further delay: the research, the policies, the reports, and the lived testimony – truth that has been buried for too long.

Stacy Bannerman. When the War Came Home: The Inside Story of Reservists and the Families They Leave Behind. New York: Continuum, 2006.

Bohnert, Amy S. B., Mark A. Ilgen, Sandro Galea, John F. McCarthy, and Frederic C. Blow. 2011. "Accidental Poisoning Mortality among Patients in the

Department of Veterans Affairs Health System." *Medical Care* **49**, no. 4 (April): 393–396. doi:10.1097/MLR.0b013e318202aa27. URL: https://doi.org/10.1097/MLR.0b013e318202aa27. Accessed August 15, 2025.

Brenner, Lisa A., Taylor A. Hostetter, Katherine A. Roenfeldt, Amy S. Hoffberg, Joshua Lusk, S. Nazem, ... Jennifer E. Forster. 2023. "Time to Suicide Death among Post-9/11 Veterans with and without Traumatic Brain Injury, Psychiatric Diagnoses, and Opioid Use Disorder." *JAMA Network Open* **6**, no. 7 (July): e2324831 (1–13). doi:10.1001/jamanetworkopen.2023.24831. URL: https://doi.org/10.1001/jamanetworkopen.2023.24831. Accessed August 15, 2025. *(Peer-reviewed original research; open-access.)*

Brown, David W., Robert F. Anda, Henning Tiemeier, Vincent J. Felitti, Valerie J. Edwards, Janet B. Croft, and Wayne H. Giles. 2009. "Adverse Childhood Experiences and the Risk of Premature Mortality." *American Journal of Preventive Medicine* **37**, no. 5 (November): 389–396. doi:10.1016/j.amepre.2009.06.021. URL: https://doi.org/10.1016/j.amepre.2009.06.021. Accessed August 15, 2025.

Bryant, Richard A., Mark L. O'Donnell, Mark Creamer, Alexander C. McFarlane, Christopher R.

Clark, and Derrick Silove. 2015. "The Psychiatric Sequelae of Traumatic Injury." *American Journal of Psychiatry* **172**, no. 3 (March): 312–320. doi:10.1176/appi.ajp.2014.14040538. URL: https://doi.org/10.1176/appi.ajp.2014.14040538. Accessed August 15, 2025.

Dube, Shanta R., Robert F. Anda, Vincent J. Felitti, Valerie J. Edwards, and Janet B. Croft. 2001. "Childhood Abuse, Household Dysfunction, and the Risk of Attempted Suicide throughout the Life Span: Findings from the Adverse Childhood Experiences Study." *JAMA* **286**, no. 24 (December): 3089–3096. doi:10.1001/jama.286.24.3089. URL: https://doi.org/10.1001/jama.286.24.3089. Accessed August 15, 2025.

Felitti, Vincent J., Robert F. Anda, Dale Nordenberg, David F. Williamson, Alison M. Spitz, Valerie Edwards, Mary P. Koss, and James S. Marks. 1998. "Relationship of Childhood Abuse and Household Dysfunction to Many of the Leading Causes of Death in Adults: The Adverse Childhood Experiences (ACE) Study." *American Journal of Preventive Medicine* **14**, no. 4 (May): 245–258. doi:10.1016/S0749-3797(98)00017-8. URL: https://doi.org/10.1016/S0749-3797(98)00017-8. Accessed August 15, 2025.

Fralick, Michael, Dharshi Thiruchelvam, Homer C. Tien, and Donald A. Redelmeier. 2019. "Association of

Traumatic Brain Injury with Suicide." *JAMA Neurology* **76**, no. 9 (September): 1021–1028. doi:10.1001/jamaneurol.2019.1311. URL: https://doi.org/10.1001/jamaneurol.2019.1311. Accessed August 15, 2025.

Hayes, Jasmeet P., Erin D. Bigler, and Mary Lou Verfaellie. 2016. "Traumatic Brain Injury as a Disorder of Brain Connectivity." *Journal of the International Neuropsychological Society* **22**, no. 2 (February): 120–137. doi:10.1017/S1355617715000740. URL: https://doi.org/10.1017/S1355617715000740. Accessed August 15, 2025.

Isaacs, Jordan Y., Michael M. Smith, Simon B. Sherry, Sherry H. Stewart, Rory M. O'Connor, and Donald H. Saklofske. 2022. "Alcohol Use and Death by Suicide: A Meta-Analysis of Thirty-Three Studies." *Suicide and Life-Threatening Behavior* **52**, no. 4 (August): 600–614. doi:10.1111/sltb.12861. URL: https://doi.org/10.1111/sltb.12861. Accessed August 15, 2025.

Magos, Andrea, and Karla Rosas. 2019. "Adverse Childhood Experiences and Combat-Related PTSD: The Importance of Early Intervention for Military Service Members." *Military Behavioral Health* 7, no. 3 (July–September): 300–309. doi:10.1080/21635781.2018.1564365. URL: https://doi.org/10.1080/21635781.2018.1564365.

Accessed August 15, 2025.

McCauley, Jenna L., Tracie Killeen, Daniel F. Gros, Kathleen T. Brady, and Sudie E. Back. 2012. "Posttraumatic Stress Disorder and Co-Occurring Substance Use Disorders: Advances in Assessment and Treatment." *Clinical Psychology: Science and Practice* **19**, no. 3 (September): 283–304. doi:10.1111/cpsp.12009. URL: https://doi.org/10.1111/cpsp.12009. Accessed August 15, 2025.

Mehic, Emir, Yufei Teng, Erik L. Antonsen, and David W. Wright. 2021. "Military Blast Exposure, Traumatic Brain Injury and Chronic Traumatic Encephalopathy: Clinical and Translational Considerations." *Frontiers in Neurology* **12** (June): 705711 (pp. 1–14). doi:10.3389/fneur.2021.705711. URL: https://doi.org/10.3389/fneur.2021.705711. Accessed August 15, 2025. *(Open-access review.)*

Pompili, Maurizio, G. Serafini, M. Innamorati, G. Dominici, S. Ferracuti, G. D. Kotzalidis, ... David Lester. 2010. "Suicidal Behavior and Alcohol Abuse." *International Journal of Environmental Research and Public Health* 7, no. 4 (April): 1392–1431. doi:10.3390/ijerph7041392. URL: https://doi.org/10.3390/ijerph7041392. Accessed August 15, 2025.

Sherin, Jonathan E., and Charles B. Nemeroff. 2011. "Post-Traumatic Stress Disorder: The Neurobiological

Impact of Psychological Trauma." *Dialogues in Clinical Neuroscience* **13**, no. 3 (September): 263–278. doi:10.31887/DCNS.2011.13.2/jsherin. URL: https://doi.org/10.31887/DCNS.2011.13.2/jsherin. Accessed August 15, 2025.

Stefan, Andrei, and Dorina Mățhe. 2016. "Psychiatric Disorders following Traumatic Brain Injury—A Cross-Sectional Study in a Neuropsychiatric Hospital." *Romanian Journal of Morphology and Embryology* **57**, no. 4 (October–December): 1295–1302. PubMed: 28174825. URL: https://pubmed.ncbi.nlm.nih.gov/28174825/. Accessed August 15, 2025.

Vasterling, Jennifer J., Mary Lou Verfaellie, and Katherine D. Sullivan. 2018. "Mild Traumatic Brain Injury and Posttraumatic Stress Disorder in Returning Veterans: Perspectives from Cognitive Neuroscience." *Clinical Psychology Review* **62** (August): 66–79. doi:10.1016/j.cpr.2018.05.002. URL: https://doi.org/10.1016/j.cpr.2018.05.002. Accessed August 15, 2025.

Yehuda, Rachel, Charles W. Hoge, Alexander C. McFarlane, Eric Vermetten, Ruth A. Lanius, Caroline M. Nievergelt, Stevan E. Hobfoll, Karestan C. Koenen, Thomas C. Neylan, and Steven E. Hyman. 2015. "Post-Traumatic Stress Disorder." *Nature Reviews Disease Primers* **1** (2015): 15057 (pp. 1–21). doi:10.1038/nrdp.2015.57. URL:

https://doi.org/10.1038/nrdp.2015.57. Accessed August 15, 2025.

Yurgil, Kate A., Daniel A. Barkauskas, Jennifer J. Vasterling, Caroline M. Nievergelt, Gerald E. Larson, Nicholas J. Schork, Brett T. Litz, William P. Nash, Dewleen G. Baker, and the Marine Resiliency Study Team. 2020. "Association between Traumatic Brain Injury and Risk of Posttraumatic Stress Disorder in Active-Duty Marines." *JAMA Psychiatry* 77, no. 1 (January): 77–87. doi:10.1001/jamapsychiatry.2019.2182. URL: https://doi.org/10.1001/jamapsychiatry.2019.2182. Accessed August 15, 2025.

Elbogen, Eric B., Sally C. Johnson, H. Ryan Wagner, Catherine Sullivan, Casey T. Taft, and Jean C. Beckham. 2014. "Violent Behaviour and Post-Traumatic Stress Disorder in U.S. Iraq and Afghanistan Veterans." *The British Journal of Psychiatry* **204**, no. 5 (May): 368–375. doi:10.1192/bjp.bp.113.134627. Accessed August 15, 2025.

Kwan, Joanna, Kimberley Sparrow, Emma Facer-Irwin, Gurvinder Thandi, Nicola T. Fear, and Deirdre MacManus. 2020. "Prevalence of Intimate Partner Violence Perpetration among Military Populations: A Systematic Review and Meta-Analysis." *Aggression and Violent Behavior* **53** (March): 101419 (pp. 1–13). doi:10.1016/j.avb.2020.101419. Accessed August 15, 2025.

Portnoy, Gena A., Matthew R. Relyea, Christine Presseau, et al. 2022. "Persistent Post-Concussion

Symptoms, Probable TBI, and Intimate Partner Violence Perpetration among Veterans: A Longitudinal Analysis." *Journal of Head Trauma Rehabilitation* **37** (Supplement): 34–42. Accessed August 15, 2025.

Rojczyk, Piotr, Christina Heller, Jennifer Seitz-Holland, et al. 2024. "Intimate Partner Violence Perpetration among Veterans: Associations with Neuropsychiatric Symptoms and Limbic Microstructure." *Frontiers in Neurology* **15** (2024): 1360424. doi:10.3389/fneur.2024.1360424. Accessed August 15, 2025.

Savarese, Victor W., Michelle K. Suvak, Laura A. King, and Daniel W. King. 2001. "Alcohol Use, Hyperarousal, and Marital Abuse in Vietnam Veterans." *Journal of Traumatic Stress* **14**, no. 4 (October): 717–732. Accessed August 15, 2025.

Schafer, Brian J. 2010. "Male Veteran Interpersonal Partner Violence (IPV) and Associated Problems." *Journal of Aggression, Maltreatment & Trauma* **19**, no. 4 (May): 414–423. doi:10.1080/10926771003799539. Accessed August 15, 2025.

Slep, Amy M. Smith, Herbert M. Foran, Richard E. Heyman, and Jeffrey D. Snarr. 2015. "Identifying Unique and Shared Risk Factors for Physical Intimate Partner Violence in the U.S. Air Force." *Aggressive Behavior* **41**, no. 3 (May–June): 227–241. Accessed August 15, 2025.

Taft, Casey T., Amy E. Street, Amy D. Marshall, Douglas J. Dowdall, and David S. Riggs. 2007. "Posttraumatic Stress Disorder, Anger, and Partner Abuse among Vietnam Combat Veterans." *Journal of Family Psychology* **21**, no. 2 (June): 270–277. Accessed August 15, 2025.

Taft, Casey T., Rebecca P. Weatherill, Heather E. Woodward, et al. 2009. "Intimate Partner and General Aggression Perpetration among Combat Veterans in a PTSD Clinic." *American Journal of Orthopsychiatry* **79**, no. 4 (October): 461–468. Accessed August 15, 2025.

Teten, Amy L., Jack A. Schumacher, Casey T. Taft, et al. 2010. "Intimate Partner Aggression Perpetrated and Sustained by Male Afghanistan, Iraq, and Vietnam Veterans with and without PTSD." *Journal of Interpersonal Violence* **25**, no. 9 (September): 1612–1630. Accessed August 15, 2025.

Farrer, Thomas J., Rebecca B. Frost, and Dawson W. Hedges. 2012. "Prevalence of Traumatic Brain Injury in Intimate Partner Violence Offenders Compared to the General Population: A Meta-Analysis." *Trauma, Violence, & Abuse* **13**, no. 2 (April): 77–82. doi:10.1177/1524838012440338. Accessed August 15, 2025.

Fals-Stewart, William, Kenneth E. Leonard, and Gordon R. Birchler. 2005. "Male-to-Female Intimate Partner Violence on Men's Drinking Days: The Moderating Effects of Antisocial Personality Disorder." *Journal of*

Consulting and Clinical Psychology **73**, no. 2 (April): 239–249. Accessed August 15, 2025.

Leonard, Kenneth E., and Brian M. Quigley. 2017. "Thirty Years of Research Show Alcohol to Be a Cause of Intimate Partner Violence." *Drug and Alcohol Review* **36**, no. 1 (January): 7–9. Accessed August 15, 2025.

Capaldi, Deborah M., Naomi B. Knoble, Jennifer W. Shortt, and Hyoun K. Kim. 2012. "A Systematic Review of Risk Factors for Intimate Partner Violence." *Partner Abuse* **3**, no. 2 (April–June): 231–280. Accessed August 15, 2025.

O'Leary, K. Daniel, Amy M. Smith Slep, and Susan G. O'Leary. 2014. "Risk Factors for Physical Violence against Partners in the United States." *Psychology of Violence* **4**, no. 1 (January): 65–77. Accessed August 15, 2025.

Stith, Sandra M., Douglas B. Smith, Casey E. Penn, David B. Ward, and Deborah Tritt. 2004. "Intimate Partner Physical Abuse Perpetration and Victimization Risk Factors: A Meta-Analytic Review." *Aggression and Violent Behavior* **10**, no. 1 (Autumn): 65–98. Accessed August 15, 2025.

Centers for Disease Control and Prevention (CDC). 2019. *Substance Use and Traumatic Brain Injury.* National Center for Injury Prevention and Control, U.S. Department of Health and Human Services. URL:

https://www.cdc.gov/traumatic-brain-injury/substance-use/index.html. Accessed August 15, 2025.

National Institute for Occupational Safety and Health (NIOSH). 2014. *Health Hazard Evaluation Report: Exposures of Helicopter Pilots and Gunners to Firearm Noise and Lead during Gunnery Target Training Exercises (HHE Report 2009-0216-3201).* U.S. Department of Health & Human Services, Centers for Disease Control and Prevention. URL: https://stacks.cdc.gov/view/cdc/172450. Accessed August 15, 2025.

Traumatic Brain Injury Center of Excellence (TBICoE). n.d. *Substance Use and TBI (Patient/Clinician Resources).* Defense Health Agency. URL: https://health.mil/TBICoE. Accessed August 15, 2025.

Traumatic Brain Injury Model Systems / MSKTC. n.d. *Alcohol Use after Traumatic Brain Injury (Factsheet).* Model Systems Knowledge Translation Center. URL: https://msktc.org/tbi/factsheets/alcohol-use-after-traumatic-brain-injury. Accessed August 15, 2025.

U.S. Department of Veterans Affairs, National Center for PTSD. n.d. *When a Child's Parent Has PTSD.* URL: https://www.ptsd.va.gov/family/effect_parent_ptsd.asp. Accessed August 15, 2025.

U.S. Department of Veterans Affairs (VA). 2013

(August). *Intimate Partner Violence: Prevalence among U.S. Military Veterans and Active Duty Servicemembers and a Review of Intervention Approaches* (VA Evidence-Based Synthesis Program Report No. 09-010). URL: https://www.hsrd.research.va.gov/publications/esp/partner_violence-REPORT.pdf. Accessed August 15, 2025.

Defense Suicide Prevention Office (DSPO) & VHA Rocky Mountain MIRECC. 2025 (March). *What You Should Know about Traumatic Brain Injury and Suicidality* (One-Pager). U.S. Department of Defense. Accessed August 15, 2025.

Department of Defense Instruction (DoDI) 1322.34. *Financial Readiness of Service Members.* Washington, DC: U.S. Department of Defense. Accessed August 15, 2025.

Department of Defense Instruction (DoDI) 1342.22. *Military Family Readiness System.* Washington, DC: U.S. Department of Defense. Accessed August 15, 2025.

Department of Defense Instruction (DoDI) 6055.01. *DoD Safety and Occupational Health (SOH) Program.* Washington, DC: U.S. Department of Defense. Accessed August 15, 2025.

Department of Defense Instruction (DoDI) 6400.06. *Domestic Abuse Involving DoD Personnel.* Washington, DC: U.S. Department of Defense. Accessed August 15, 2025.

Department of Defense Instruction (DoDI) 6490.04. *Mental Health Evaluations of Members of the Military Services.* Washington, DC: U.S. Department of Defense. Accessed August 15, 2025.

Department of Defense Instruction (DoDI) 6490.13. *Comprehensive Policy on Neurocognitive (TBI-Related) Assessment/Management.* Washington, DC: U.S. Department of Defense. Accessed August 15, 2025.

Powell, Jeffrey R., et al. 2020. "Neuroinflammatory Biomarkers Associated with Mild Traumatic Brain Injury History in Special Operations Forces Combat Soldiers." *Journal of Head Trauma Rehabilitation* **35**, no. 5 (September–October): 294–304. Accessed August 15, 2025.

Richman, Mitch. 2022 (February 8). "Teasing Out the Effects of Blasts on Mental Health." *VA Research Currents.* U.S. Department of Veterans Affairs. URL: https://www.research.va.gov/currents/0222-Teasing-out-the-effects-of-blasts-on-mental-health.cfm. Accessed August 15, 2025.

Rowland, Jordan A., and Sarah L. Martindale. 2024. "Considerations for the Assessment of Blast Exposure in Service Members and Veterans." *Frontiers in Neurology* **15**: 1383710 (pp. 1–17). doi:10.3389/fneur.2024.1383710. URL: https://doi.org/10.3389/fneur.2024.1383710. Accessed August 15, 2025.

Beydoun, Hind A., May A. Beydoun, Jay S.

Kaufman, Brenda Lo, and Alan B. Zonderman. 2012. "Intimate Partner Violence against Adult Women and Its Association with Major Depressive Disorder, Depressive Symptoms, and Postpartum Depression: A Systematic Review and Meta-Analysis." *Social Science & Medicine* **75**, no. 6 (September): 959–975. doi:10.1016/j.socscimed.2012.04.025. Accessed August 15, 2025.

Cerulli, Catherine, Robert M. Bossarte, and Melissa E. Dichter. 2014. "Exploring Intimate Partner Violence Status among Male Veterans and Associated Health Outcomes." *American Journal of Men's Health* **8**, no. 1 (January): 66–73. doi:10.1177/1557988313492558. Accessed August 15, 2025.

Cerulli, Catherine, Robert M. Bossarte, Melissa E. Dichter, and Amy Madsen. 2014. "Examining the Intersection between Suicidal Behaviors and Intimate Partner Violence among a Sample of Males Receiving Services from the Veterans Health Administration." *American Journal of Men's Health* **8**, no. 5 (September): 440–443. doi:10.1177/1557988314522828. Accessed August 15, 2025.

Daugherty, Jessica C., Javier Verdejo-Román, Miguel Pérez-García, and Natalia Hidalgo-Ruzzante. 2022. "The Spectrum of Structural Brain Alterations in Female Survivors of Intimate Partner Violence." *Journal of Interpersonal Violence* **37**, nos. 7–8:

NP4684–NP4717. doi:10.1177/0886260520959621. Accessed August 15, 2025.

Daugherty, Jessica C., María García-Navas-Menchero, Carmen Fernández-Fillol, Natalia Hidalgo-Ruzzante, and Miguel Pérez-García. 2024. "Tentative Causes of Brain and Neuropsychological Alterations in Women Victims"

Daugherty, Jessica C., María García-Navas-Menchero, Carmen Fernández-Fillol, Natalia Hidalgo-Ruzzante, and Miguel Pérez-García. 2024. "Tentative Causes of Brain and Neuropsychological Alterations in Women Victims of Intimate Partner Violence." *Brain Sciences* **14**, no. 10 (October): 996 (pp. 1–22). doi:10.3390/brainsci14100996. Accessed August 15, 2025.

Gerlock, April A., Jana G. Szarka, Karen Cox, and Ofer Harel. 2016. "Comparing Intimately Violent to Non-Violent Veterans in Treatment for Posttraumatic Stress Disorder." *Journal of Family Violence* **31**, no. 6 (August): 667–678. doi:10.1007/s10896-016-9822-6. Accessed August 15, 2025.

Miles, Sarah R., David S. Menefee, Jessica Wanner, Amanda L. Teten Tharp, and Thomas A. Kent. 2016. "The Relationship between Emotion Dysregulation and Impulsive Aggression in Veterans with Posttraumatic Stress Disorder Symptoms." *Journal of Interpersonal Violence* **31**, no. 10 (June): 1795–1816. doi:10.1177/0886260515570746.

Accessed August 15, 2025.

Fanning, Jennifer R., Royce Lee, and Emil F. Coccaro. 2016. "Comorbid Intermittent Explosive Disorder and Posttraumatic Stress Disorder: Clinical Correlates and Relationship to Suicidal Behavior." *Comprehensive Psychiatry* **70** (June): 125–133. doi:10.1016/j.comppsych.2016.05.018. Accessed August 15, 2025.

Monson, Candice M., Joseph L. Price, Brian F. Rodriguez, Michael P. Ripley, and Richard A. Warner. 2004. "Emotional Deficits in Military-Related PTSD: An Investigation of Content and Process Disturbances." *Journal of Traumatic Stress* **17**, no. 3 (June): 275–279. doi:10.1023/B:JOTS.0000029271.58494.05. Accessed August 15, 2025.

Simmons, Alan N., Martin P. Paulus, Susan R. Thorp, Scott C. Matthews, Sonya B. Norman, and Murray B. Stein. 2008. "Functional Activation and Neural Networks in Women with Posttraumatic Stress Disorder Related to Intimate Partner Violence." *Biological Psychiatry* **64**, no. 8 (October): 681–690. doi:10.1016/j.biopsych.2008.05.027. Accessed August 15, 2025.

Lester, Patricia, Kris Peterson, James Reeves, Larry Knauss, Dorie Glover, Catherine Mogil, Naihua Duan, William Saltzman, Robert Pynoos,

Katherine Wilt, and William Beardslee. 2010. "The Long War and Parental Combat Deployment: Effects on Military Children and At-Home Spouses." *Journal of the American Academy of Child & Adolescent Psychiatry* **49**, no. 4 (April): 310–320. doi:10.1016/j.jaac.2010.01.003. (Erratum: 2012, **51**[3], 337.) Accessed August 15, 2025.

Collins, Elizabeth M. 2015 (May 6). "Experts Explain Mental State of Military Children." *U.S. Army / Soldiers Magazine.* Includes "Parents with Invisible Wounds" remarks by Michael Faran, M.D., and Stephen Cozza, M.D. URL: https://www.army.mil/article/147786/. Accessed August 15, 2025.

National Alliance for Caregiving & United Health Foundation. 2010 (November). *Caregivers of Veterans—Serving on the Homefront: Report of Study Findings.* Washington, DC. (Full report PDF available.) Accessed August 15, 2025.

Shepherd-Banigan, Megan, Sophia R. Sherman, Jennifer H. Lindquist, Karen E. M. Miller, Megan Tucker, Valerie A. Smith, and Courtney H. Van Houtven. 2020. "Family Caregivers of Veterans Experience High Levels of Burden, Distress, and Financial Strain." *Journal of the American Geriatrics Society* **68**, no. 11 (November): 2675–2683. doi:10.1111/jgs.16767. Accessed August 15, 2025.

Bohnert, Amy S. B., Mark A. Ilgen, Sandro Galea, John F. McCarthy, and Frederic C. Blow. 2011.

"Accidental Poisoning Mortality among Patients in the Department of Veterans Affairs Health System." *Medical Care* **49**, no. 4 (April): 393–396. doi:10.1097/MLR.0b013e318202aa27. Accessed August 15, 2025.

Fox, Victoria, Christina Dalman, Huan Song, Anna-Clara Hollander, James B. Kirkbride, and Amy E. Pitman. 2021. "Suicide Risk in People with Post-Traumatic Stress Disorder: A Cohort Study of 3.1 Million People in Sweden." *Journal of Affective Disorders* **279** (February): 609–616. doi:10.1016/j.jad.2020.10.009. Accessed August 15, 2025.

Isaacs, Jordan Y., Michael M. Smith, Simon B. Sherry, Sherry H. Stewart, Rory M. O'Connor, and Donald H. Saklofske. 2022. "Alcohol Use and Death by Suicide: A Meta-Analysis of Thirty-Three Studies." *Suicide and Life-Threatening Behavior* **52**, no. 4 (August): 600–614. doi:10.1111/sltb.12861. Accessed August 15, 2025.

Kaplan, Michael S., Nathalie Huguet, Bentson H. McFarland, and Juncheng Cao. 2014. "Use of Alcohol before Suicide in the United States." *American Journal of Preventive Medicine* **46**, no. 3 (March): 300–304. doi:10.1016/j.amepre.2013.11.007. Accessed August 15, 2025.

Skipper, Lanny D., Robert D. Forsten, Eun-Ho Kim, John D. Wilk, and Charles W. Hoge. 2014. "Relationship of Combat Experiences and Alcohol Misuse among U.S. Special Operations Soldiers." *Military Medicine* **179**, no. 3 (March): 301–308. doi:10.7205/MILMED-D-13-00400. Accessed August 15, 2025.

National Institute on Drug Abuse (NIDA). 2019 (October 23). *Substance Use and Military Life (DrugFacts).* Bethesda, MD: National Institutes of Health. URL: https://nida.nih.gov/publications/drugfacts/substance-use-military-life. Accessed August 15, 2025.

Riley, Rachael. 2023 (January 11). "Fifteen U.S. Army Special Operations Command Soldiers Questioned during Fort Bragg Drug Probe." *The Fayetteville Observer* (USA TODAY Network). Accessed August 15, 2025.

Harp, Seth. 2023 (February 15). "Pentagon Finally Stops Hiding Military Overdose Epidemic." *Rolling Stone.* Accessed August 15, 2025.

Taft, Casey T., Amy A. Macdonald, Richard J. Musser, Joseph R. Moore, Michael M. Shnaider, Niloofar Monson, Galina A. Portnoy, and Katherine M. Murphy. 2016. "Strength at Home Men's Program to Prevent Posttraumatic Stress Disorder-Related Domestic Violence in Military Veterans: A Randomized Clinical Trial." *The Journal of Clinical Psychiatry* 77, no. 9 (September): 1168–1175. doi:10.4088/JCP.15m10174. Accessed August 15, 2025.

Back, Sudie E., Therese K. Killeen, Daniel F. Gros, Lori Keyser-Marcus, Kristina R. Payne, Kelley A.

Williams, Katherine T. Brady, and Jenna L. McCauley. 2018. "A Randomized Clinical Trial of 'Concurrent Treatment of PTSD and Substance Use Disorders Using Prolonged Exposure (COPE)' in Military Veterans." *Addictive Behaviors* **90** (July): 369–377. doi:10.1016/j.addbeh.2018.01.020. (Open-access author manuscript available.) Accessed August 15, 2025.

Department of Veterans Affairs & Department of Defense (VA/DoD). 2021 (Version 3.0). *Clinical Practice Guideline for the Management and Rehabilitation of Post-Acute Mild Traumatic Brain Injury*. Washington, DC. (PDF available via Health.mil.) Accessed August 15, 2025.

Swensen, Eric. 2023 (December 6). "Study: Repeated Blast Exposure Increases Brain Inflammation." *UVA Today / UVA Health Newsroom*. Accessed August 15, 2025.

Powell, Jeffrey R., et al. 2020. "Neuroinflammatory Biomarkers Associated with Mild Traumatic Brain Injury History in Special Operations Forces Combat Soldiers." *Journal of Head Trauma Rehabilitation* **35**, no. 5 (September–October): 294–304. Accessed August 15, 2025.

Frueh, B. Christopher, Anusha Madan, John C. Fowler, Susan Stomberg, Matthew Bradshaw, Kristen Kelly, Beth Weinstein, Michael Luttrell, Susan G. Danner, and Debra C. Beidel. 2020. "'Operator Syndrome': A Unique Constellation of Medical and Behavioral Health-Care Needs of Military Special Operation Forces." *International Journal of Psychiatry in*

Medicine **55**, no. 4 (August): 281–295. doi:10.1177/0091217420906659. Accessed August 15, 2025.

Dieter, J. N. I., and S. D. Engel. 2019. "Traumatic Brain Injury and Posttraumatic Stress Disorder: Comorbid Consequences of War." *Neuroscience Insights* **14**: 1179069519892933 (pp. 1–17). doi:10.1177/1179069519892933. Accessed August 15, 2025.

Iverson, Katherine M., and Tanya K. Pogoda. 2015. "Traumatic Brain Injury among Women Veterans: An Invisible Wound of Intimate Partner Violence." *Medical Care* **53**, no. 4 (Suppl 1, April): S112–S119. doi:10.1097/MLR.0000000000000263. Accessed August 15, 2025.

Iverson, Katherine M., Crystal M. Dardis, and Tanya K. Pogoda. 2017. "Traumatic Brain Injury and PTSD Symptoms as a Consequence of Intimate Partner Violence." *Comprehensive Psychiatry* **74** (August): 80–87. doi:10.1016/j.comppsych.2017.01.013. Accessed August 15, 2025.

Haag, Heidi L., Dana Jones, Tonia Joseph, and Angela Colantonio. 2019/2022. "Battered and Brain Injured: Traumatic Brain Injury among Women Survivors of Intimate Partner Violence—A Scoping Review." *Trauma, Violence, & Abuse* **23**, no. 4 (October 2022): 1270–1287. doi:10.1177/1524838019850623. (Epub 2019.) Accessed August 15, 2025.

Murray, Christine E., Kelli Lundgren, Laura N. Olson, and Gretchen Hunnicutt. 2016. "Practice Update: What Professionals Who Are Not Brain Injury Specialists Need to Know about Intimate Partner Violence-Related Traumatic Brain Injury." *Trauma, Violence, & Abuse* **17**, no. 3 (July): 298–305. doi:10.1177/1524838015584364. Accessed August 15, 2025.

Iverson, Katherine M., Katherine H. Iverson, Rebecca K. Kimerling, et al. 2024. "Prevalence of Past-Year Intimate Partner Violence and Sexual Violence among Veterans." *Journal of General Internal Medicine* **39**, Suppl 1 (2024): S54–S62. doi:10.1007/s11606-024-08703-6. Accessed August 15, 2025.

Foran, Heather M., and K. Daniel O'Leary. 2008. "Alcohol and Intimate Partner Violence: A Meta-Analytic Review." *Clinical Psychology Review* **28**, no. 7 (November): 1222–1234. doi:10.1016/j.cpr.2008.05.001. Accessed August 15, 2025.

Foran, Heather M., Richard E. Heyman, Amy M. Smith Slep, and Jeffrey D. Snarr. 2012. "Hazardous Alcohol Use and Intimate Partner Violence in the Military: Understanding Protective Factors." *Psychology of Addictive Behaviors* **26**, no. 3 (September): 471–483. Accessed August 15, 2025.

Chermack, Stephen T., and Frederic C. Blow. 2002. "Violence among Patients in Substance Abuse Treatment: A Review of the Literature." *Aggression and Violent Behavior*

7, no. 4 (July–August): 415–432. doi:10.1016/S1359-1789(01)00081-0. Accessed August 15, 2025.

Jowers, Karen. 2021 (May 7). "How Bad Is DoD's Domestic Abuse Problem? Unclear, Thanks to Data Gaps, Auditors Say." *Military Times*. Accessed August 15, 2025.

Lawrence, Quil. 2016 (April 17). "After Combat Stress, Violence Can Show Up at Home." *NPR News* (with Alaska Public Media reprint). Accessed August 15, 2025.

Kappell, Jacob. 2019 (December 4). *Military Families and Intimate Partner Violence: Background and Issues for Congress* (CRS Report R46097). Congressional Research Service. Accessed August 15, 2025.

Napolitano, Donna. 2015. *Childhood Disrupted: How Your Biography Becomes Your Biology, and How You Can Heal.* New York, NY: Atria Books. Accessed August 15, 2025.

Schafer, Andrew. 2017. *Generations of War: The Rise of the Warrior Caste & the All-Volunteer Force.* Washington, DC: Center for a New American Security. Accessed August 15, 2025.

Small Wars Journal. 2017 (May 8). "CNAS Releases New Report 'Generations of War: The Rise of the Warrior Caste & the All-Volunteer Force.'" Accessed August 15, 2025.

Substance Abuse and Mental Health Services Administration (SAMHSA). 2016. *Substance Abuse* *and Suicide Prevention: Evidence and Implications—A White Paper (SMA-16-4935)*. Rockville, MD. Accessed August 15, 2025.

Arnon, Shay, Prudence W. Fisher, Alison Pickover, Ari Lowell, J. Blake Turner, Anne Hilburn, Jody Jacob-McVey, et al. 2020. "Equine-Assisted Therapy for Veterans with PTSD: Manual Development and Preliminary Findings." *Military Medicine* **185**, nos. 5–6 (June): e557–e564. doi:10.1093/milmed/usz444. Accessed August 15, 2025.

Fisher, Prudence W., Yuval Neria, D. Pelcovitz, et al. 2021. "Equine-Assisted Therapy for Posttraumatic Stress Disorder among Military Veterans: An Open Trial." *The Journal of Clinical Psychiatry* **82**, no. 6 (2021): 21m14145. doi:10.4088/JCP.21m14145. Accessed August 15, 2025.

Appel, Anne E., and George W. Holden. 1998. "The Co-Occurrence of Spouse and Physical Child Abuse: A Review and Appraisal." *Journal of Family Psychology* **12**, no. 4 (December): 578–599. doi:10.1037/0893-3200.12.4.578. URL: https://doi.org/10.1037/0893-3200.12.4.578. Accessed August 15, 2025.__EBSCO OpenURL

Pearson, Isabelle, Sabrina Page, Cathy Zimmerman, Franziska Meinck, Floriza Gennari, Alessandra Guedes, and Heidi Stöckl. 2023 (epub 2022). "The Co-Occurrence of Intimate Partner Violence and Violence Against Children: A Systematic Review on Associated Factors in Low- and Middle-Income Countries." *Trauma, Violence, & Abuse* 24, no. 4 (October): 2097–2114. doi:10.1177/15248380221082943. URL: https://pubmed.ncbi.nlm.nih.gov/35481390/. Accessed August 15, 2025.

Winnicott, D. W. (1960). The theory of the parent–infant relationship. *International Journal of Psycho-Analysis, 41,* 585–595. PMID: 13785877._PubMedtcf-website-media-library.s3.eu-west-2.amazonaws.com

Schore, A. N. (2001). Effects of a secure attachment relationship on right brain development, affect regulation, and infant mental health. *Infant Mental Health Journal, 22*(1–2), 7–66. https://doi.org/10.1002/1097-0355(200101/04)22:1<7::AID-IMHJ2>3.0.CO;2-N._Wiley Online Library

Levendosky, A. A., Bogat, G. A., Lonstein, J. S., Martinez-Torteya, C., Muzik, M., Granger, D. A., & von Eye, A. (2016). Infant adrenocortical reactivity and behavioral functioning: Relation to early exposure to maternal intimate partner violence. *Stress, 19*(1), 37–44. https://doi.org/10.3109/10253890.2015.1108303._ PubMedPMC

Martinez-Torteya, C., Bogat, G. A., Lonstein, J. S., Granger, D. A., & Levendosky, A. A. (2017). Exposure to intimate partner violence *in utero* and infant internalizing behaviors: Moderation by salivary cortisol–

alpha amylase asymmetry. *Early Human Development, 113*, 40–48. https://doi.org/10.1016/j.earlhumdev.2017.07.014. PubMedPMC

Scheeringa, M. S., Myers, L., Putnam, F. W., & Zeanah, C. H. (2012). Diagnosing PTSD in early childhood: An empirical assessment of four approaches. *Journal of Traumatic Stress, 25*(4), 359–367. https://doi.org/10.1002/jts.21723. PubMedPMC

Knipe, Duleeka; Vallis, Emma; Kendall, Luke; Snow, Martha; Kirkpatrick, Kyla; Jarvis, Rosie; Metcalfe, Chris; Eisenstadt, Nathan; Bickham, Viv. (2024). Suicide rates in high-risk, high-harm perpetrators of domestic abuse in England and Wales. *Crisis, 45*(3), 242–245. https://doi.org/10.1027/0227-5910/a000925. PMID: 37606346. Accessed August 15, 2025. PubMed

Kafka, Julie M.; Moracco, Kathryn E.; Taheri, Caroline; Young, Belinda-Rose; Graham, Laurie M.; Macy, Rebecca J.; Proescholdbell, Scott. (2022). Intimate partner violence victimization and perpetration as precursors to suicide. *SSM – Population Health, 18*, 101079. https://doi.org/10.1016/j.ssmph.2022.101079. PMCID: PMC8968650. Accessed August 15, 2025. PubMed

Graham, Laurie M.; Kafka, Julie M.; AbiNader, Millan A. (2025). Co-occurrence of intimate partner violence and suicide mortality among adolescents and young adults in the United States. *Journal of Adolescent*

Health, 76(2), 283–290. https://doi.org/10.1016/j.jadohealth.2024.09.019. PMID: 39453344. Epub 2024 Oct 28. Accessed August 15, 2025. PubMedJah Online

Thackeray, Jonathan D., et al.; Council on Child Abuse and Neglect; Council on Injury, Violence, and Poison Prevention; American Academy of Pediatrics. 2023. "Intimate Partner Violence: Role of the Pediatrician." *Pediatrics* **152**, no. 1 (July): e2023062509. doi:10.1542/peds.2023-062509. URL: https://pubmed.ncbi.nlm.nih.gov/37337842/. Accessed August 15, 2025._PubMedvirginiapediatrics.org

Burnett-Zeigler, I., Ilgen, M., Valenstein, M., Zivin, K., Gorman, L., Blow, A. J., & Blow, F. C. (2011). *Prevalence and correlates of alcohol misuse among returning Afghanistan and Iraq veterans.* Addictive Behaviors, 36(8), 801–806. https://doi.org/10.1016/j.addbeh.2011.03.007

Herman, J. L. (1992). *Complex PTSD: A syndrome in survivors of prolonged and repeated trauma.* Journal of Traumatic Stress, 5(3), 377–391. https://doi.org/10.1002/jts.2490050305

Gewirtz, A. H., Erbes, C. R., Polusny, M. A., Forgatch, M. S., & DeGarmo, D. S. (2010). *Helping military families through the deployment process: Strategies to support parenting.* Professional Psychology: Research and Practice, 41(1), 8–16.

https://doi.org/10.1037/a0018195

Lester, P., Peterson, K., Reeves, J., Knauss, L., Glover, D., Mogil, C., ... Beardslee, W. (2010). *The long war and parental combat deployment: Effects on military children and at-home spouses.* Journal of the American Academy of Child & Adolescent Psychiatry, 49(4), 310–320. https://doi.org/10.1016/j.jaac.2010.01.003

Cloitre, M., Garvert, D. W., Brewin, C. R., Bryant, R. A., & Maercker, A. (2014). *Evidence for proposed ICD-11 PTSD and complex PTSD: A latent profile analysis.* European Journal of Psychotraumatology, 5(1), 25097. https://doi.org/10.3402/ejpt.v5.25097

Frewen, P. A., Lanius, R. A., Dozois, D. J. A., Neufeld, R. W. J., Pain, C., Hopper, J. W., Densmore, M., & Stevens, T. K. (2008). *Clinical and neural correlates of alexithymia in posttraumatic stress disorder.* Journal of Abnormal Psychology, 117(1), 171–181. https://doi.org/10.1037/0021-843X.117.1.171

Cozza, S. J., Haskins, R., & Lerner, R. M. (2019). ***Military and veteran families and children:*** *Policies and programs for health maintenance and positive development.* The Future of Children, 29(1), 139–162. https://doi.org/10.1353/foc.2019.0006

Chandra, A., Lara-Cinisomo, S., Jaycox, L. H., Tanielian, T., Burns, R. M., Ruder, T., & Han, B. (2013). *Children on the homefront: The experience of* *children from military families*. Pediatrics, 131(6), 1009–1016. https://doi.org/10.1542/peds.2012-0115

Cozza, S. J., & Lerner, R. M. (2013). *Military children and families: Introducing the issue*. The Future of Children, 23(2), 3–11. https://doi.org/10.1353/foc.2013.0013

Felitti, V. J., Anda, R. F., Nordenberg, D., Williamson, D. F., Spitz, A. M., Edwards, V., Koss, M. P., & Marks, J. S. (1998). *Relationship of childhood abuse and household dysfunction to many of the leading causes of death in adults: The Adverse Childhood Experiences (ACE) Study*. American Journal of Preventive Medicine, 14(4), 245–258. https://doi.org/10.1016/S0749-3797(98)00017-8

Helmreich, I., Kunzler, A., Chmitorz, A., König, J., Binder, H., Wessa, M., & Lieb, K. (2011). *Alexithymia and the processing of emotional stimuli in post-traumatic stress disorder*. Journal of Affective Disorders, 132(3), 373–381. https://doi.org/10.1016/j.jad.2011.03.018

Brain Injury Association of America. n.d. *Traumatic Brain Injury Fact Sheet.* https://biausa.org/brain-injury-fact-sheet.

Coccaro, Emil F., Royce Lee, and Michael S. McCloskey. 2016. "Intermittent Explosive Disorder and Aggression." *Frontiers in Behavioral Neuroscience* 10: 86. https://pmc.ncbi.nlm.nih.gov/articles/PMC5024714/.

Defense Suicide Prevention Office. 2025. *What You Should Know about Traumatic Brain Injury and Suicide Prevention.* March 11, 2025. https://www.dspo.mil/Portals/113/Documents/20250311-DSPO-TBI-and-Suicidality-One-Pager-508c.pdf.

Fish, Lauren, and Paul Scharre. 2018. *Protecting Warfighters from Blast Injury*. Washington, DC: Center for a New American Security. https://www.cnas.org/publications/reports/protecting-warfighters-from-blast-injury.

Griffiths, Meredith. 2011. "Combat Affects the Brain's Fight–Flight Complex." *ABC Science,* August 31, 2011. https://www.abc.net.au/science/articles/2011/08/31/3306680.htm.

Mosti, Caterina, Emil F. Coccaro, and Erin A. Hazlett. 2018. "Mild Traumatic Brain Injury, Aggression, Impulsivity, and a History of Other- and Self-Directed Aggression." *Journal of Neuropsychiatry and Clinical Neurosciences* 30 (2): 85–94. https://pubmed.ncbi.nlm.nih.gov/29505319/.

Powell, Jacob Robert. 2020. "The Neurophysiological Effects of Blast Exposure and Mild Traumatic Brain Injury in Special Operations Soldiers." PhD diss., University of North Carolina at Chapel Hill. https://cdr.lib.unc.edu/concern/dissertations/h702qh49f?locale=en.

Powell, Jacob R., Laura Saba, Robert M. McCarron, et al. 2020. "Neuroinflammatory Biomarkers Associated with Mild Traumatic Brain Injury History in Special Operations Combat Soldiers." *Journal of Neurotrauma* 37 (18): 1980–87. https://pubmed.ncbi.nlm.nih.gov/32881763/.

Stone, James R., Rohan Patel, and Flora M. Hammond. 2023. "Neurological Effects of Repeated Blast Exposure in Special Operations Personnel." *Journal of Neurotrauma* 40 (1–2): 129–40. https://pubmed.ncbi.nlm.nih.gov/37950709/.

Washington, Nicole. 2020. "Living with Memory Loss as a Symptom of PTSD." *Healthline,* July 31, 2020. https://www.healthline.com/health/mental-health/memory-loss-and-ptsd.

Zhang, L., K. Wang, C. Zhu, F. Yu, H. Chen, and J. Tian. 2022. "Dynamic Changes in Brain Structure in Patients with Post-Traumatic Stress Disorder after Motor Vehicle Accidents: A Voxel-Based Morphometry Study." *Journal of Affective Disorders* 315: 109–16. https://pubmed.ncbi.nlm.nih.gov/36275224/.

Institute for Women's Policy Research. *Domestic Violence and Economic Security: Barriers to and Opportunities for Economic Independence after Abuse.* Washington, DC: IWPR, 2020. https://iwpr.org/wp-content/uploads/2020/11/B362-Domestic-Violence-and-Economic-Security.pdf.

Bellotti, Elisa, Mario Paolucci, and Federica Zaccaria. "Personal Networks of Intimate Partner Violence Victims: A Mixed-Methods Analysis of Network Support and Hindrance." *Frontiers in Psychology* 12 (2021). https://doi.org/10.3389/fpsyg.2021.765411.

Bannerman, Stacy. "High Risk of Military Domestic Violence on the Home Front." *SFGate*, April 7, 2014. https://www.sfgate.com/opinion/article/high-risk-of-military-domestic-violence-on-the-5377562.php. Accessed August 16, 2025.

Bannerman, Stacy. "The Fatal 'New Normal' for Wives of Veterans." *Women's Media Center*, March 8, 2017. https://womensmediacenter.com/news-features/the-fatal-new-normal-for-wives-of-veterans. Accessed August 16, 2025.

Bannerman, Stacy. "Advocates Bring Action Against Pentagon for Service-Related Domestic Violence." *Women's Media Center*, May 19, 2025. https://womensmediacenter.com/articles/entry/advocates-bring-action-against-pentagon-for-service-related-domestic-violence. Accessed August 16, 2025.

Bannerman, Stacy (interview with David Masciotra). "When It Comes to Military Service-Connected Domestic Violence, Silence Is Deadly." *Washington Monthly*, June 25, 2025.

https://washingtonmonthly.com/2025/06/25/when-it-comes-to-military-service-connected-domestic-violence-silence-is-deadly. Accessed August 16, 2025.

Kime, Patricia. "Military Domestic Violence Convictions Skyrocketed After Commanders Were Removed from the Process." *Military.com*, June 24, 2025. https://www.military.com/daily-news/investigations-and-features/2025/06/24/military-domestic-violence-convictions-skyrocketed-after-commanders-were-removed-process.html. Accessed August 16, 2025.

Associated Press. "Army Sergeant Charged with Attempted Murder in the Shootings of 5 Fort Stewart Soldiers." *Associated Press*, February 6, 2025. https://apnews.com/article/ef534ecf73300b21c2bb2091e45c2dfc. Accessed August 16, 2025.

Washington Post Lamothe, Dan. "Army Ranger Accused of Raping, Assaulting Women He Met on Dating Apps." *Washington Post*, June 9, 2025. https://www.washingtonpost.com/national-security/2025/06/09/army-ranger-rape-trial. Accessed August 16, 2025.

Task & Purpose Snow, Shawn. "Army Audit Shows Thousands of Domestic Abuse Cases Went Uncounted, Raising Accountability Concerns." *Task & Purpose*, October 25, 2022. https://taskandpurpose.com/news/army-audit-domestic-abuse-cases. Accessed August 16, 2025.

Project on Government Oversight (POGO) Wood, Danielle. "Thousands of Army Domestic Abuse Incidents Uncounted, Audit Shows." *Project on Government Oversight (POGO),* November 3, 2022. https://www.pogo.org/investigations/thousands-of-army-domestic-abuse-incidents-uncounted-audit-shows. Accessed August 16, 2025.

U.S. Department of the Air Force. "Department of the Air Force Review to Improve Domestic Violence Support to Victims." *U.S. Air Force/Space Force News,* January 30, 2023. https://www.spaceforce.mil/News/Article-Display/Article/3281269/department-of-the-air-force-review-to-improve-domestic-violence-support-to-vict. Accessed August 16, 2025.

Gillibrand, Kirsten. "Gillibrand Touts Success of Her Military Justice Legislation as Report Finds an Increase in Domestic Violence Convictions in the Armed Services." *Office of Senator Kirsten Gillibrand,* June 24, 2025. https://www.gillibrand.senate.gov/news/press/release/gillibrand-touts-success-of-her-military-justice-legislation-as-report-finds-an-increase-in-domestic-violence-convictions-in-the-armed-services. Accessed August 16, 2025.

Glossary

ACE (Adverse Childhood Experiences)

Stressful or traumatic events that happen before age 18, such as abuse, neglect, or growing up with addiction or violence at home. The higher a person's ACE score, the greater their risk for health problems later in life, including depression, PTSD, and substance abuse.

ASAP (Army Substance Abuse Program)

A program run by the Army to prevent and treat alcohol and drug misuse. While it exists on paper, soldiers and families often describe it as inconsistent or ineffective.

BWE (Blast Wave Exposure)

Damage to the brain caused by repeated exposure to shockwaves from explosions (like breaching doors, firing heavy weapons, or being near blasts). Unlike a concussion from hitting your head, BWE can harm the brain without any physical impact.

C-PTSD (Complex Post-Traumatic Stress Disorder)

A severe form of PTSD that develops after repeated trauma over time (such as combat deployments or ongoing abuse). Symptoms can include emotional numbness, constant hyper-alertness, anger, and trouble maintaining relationships.

CID (Criminal Investigation Division)

The Army's own investigative branch—similar to the FBI but for soldiers. They handle serious crimes within the Army, including assault, abuse, and homicide.

DARVO (Deny, Attack, Reverse Victim and Offender)
A tactic used by abusers: first deny the abuse, then attack the credibility of the person speaking out, and finally claim to be the "real victim."

DoD (Department of Defense)

The U.S. government agency in charge of the military (Army, Navy, Air Force, Marines, Space Force). It makes and enforces policies that affect service members and their families.

DoDI (Department of Defense Instruction)

A formal rulebook issued by the DoD. These instructions set mandatory policies for commanders and families (for example, how to handle domestic abuse or brain health screenings). The problem is that many of these policies aren't enforced in practice.

FAP (Family Advocacy Program)

The military's program meant to prevent and respond to domestic violence and child abuse within military families.

Many spouses have never even been told it exists, or don't know how to access it safely.

GAL (Guardian ad Litem)

A lawyer appointed by the court to represent a child's best interests in custody disputes or abuse cases. A GAL isn't the child's personal lawyer—they're supposed to act as a neutral investigator and advocate.

GWOT (Global War on Terror)

The military campaigns that began after the September 11, 2001 attacks. These wars led to repeated deployments for Special Operations soldiers, with heavy mental and physical costs for service members and families.

IDC (Incident Determination Committee)

A panel within the military that reviews cases of domestic violence or child abuse and decides whether the allegations are "substantiated." Even when abuse is confirmed, military commands don't always act on these findings.

IPV (Intimate Partner Violence)

Another term for domestic violence—physical, sexual, or emotional abuse between partners or spouses.

MOS (Military Occupational Specialty)

The specific job a soldier has in the Army (for example,

medic, mechanic, or Green Beret). Certain jobs, especially in Special Operations, carry much higher risks of brain injury and combat trauma.

OPTEMPO (Operational Tempo)

Military jargon for the pace and intensity of training, deployments, and missions. A high OPTEMPO means soldiers are almost constantly gone or preparing to leave again. Families often describe this as living in survival mode.

Operator Syndrome

A term used to describe the cluster of physical, psychological, and social problems seen in Special Operations veterans. It combines brain injury, PTSD, hormone changes, sleep issues, chronic pain, and strained relationships.

PTSD (Post-Traumatic Stress Disorder)

A mental health condition triggered by traumatic events (like combat or assault). Symptoms include nightmares, flashbacks, hypervigilance, rage, emotional numbness, and difficulty trusting others.

SFRG (Soldier and Family Readiness Group)

An Army program meant to support military families during deployments and crises. In reality, leaders often aren't trained to deal with serious issues like domestic violence, leaving families without real help.

SOF (Special Operations Forces)

Elite U.S. military units trained for dangerous missions—like the Army Special Forces ("Green Berets"), Navy SEALs, Air Force Special Tactics, and the 160th SOAR (Night Stalkers). These soldiers face some of the highest risks for brain injury and combat trauma.

SUD (Substance Use Disorder)

The medical term for addiction to alcohol or drugs. In soldiers, it often develops alongside PTSD or brain injury, creating a "deadly trifecta."

TBI (Traumatic Brain Injury)

An injury to the brain caused by a blow to the head, blast wave, or repeated concussions. Symptoms can include memory loss, mood swings, headaches, poor impulse control, and aggression.

VA (Department of Veterans Affairs)

The federal agency responsible for providing health care and benefits to veterans. It is often criticized for long wait times, limited access, and failure to address combat-related injuries effectively.

Amen.

www.blacksmithpublishing.com

www.ingramcontent.com/pod-product-compliance
Lightning Source LLC
Chambersburg PA
CBHW020416150626
46554CB00014B/1639
9781956904260